e-Marketing

Improving Marketing Effectiveness in a Digital World

Malcolm McDonald and Hugh Wilson

School of Management

PEARSON EDUCATION LIMITED

Head Office:
Edinburgh Gate
Harlow CM20 2JE
Tel: +44 (0)1279 623623
Fax: +44 (0)1279 431059

London Office:
128 Long Acre, London WC2E 9AN
Tel: +44 (0)171 447 2000
Fax: +44 (0)171 240 5771
Website: www.business-minds.com

First published in Great Britain 1999

© Pearson Education Limited 1999

The right of Malcolm McDonald and Hugh Wilson to be identified as authors
of this work has been asserted by them in accordance
with the Copyright, Designs, and Patents Act 1988.

ISBN 0 273 64427 0

British Library Cataloguing in Publication Data
A CIP catalogue record for this book can be obtained from the British Library.

10 9 8 7 6 5 4 3

Typeset by Boyd Elliott Typesetting
Printed and bound in Great Britain

The Publishers' policy is to use paper manufactured from sustainable forests.

About the authors

Malcolm H. B. McDonald MA(Oxon), MSc, PhD, FCIM, FRSA is a Professor of Marketing Strategy and Deputy Director of Cranfield School of Management with special responsibility for external affairs.

He is a graduate in English Language and Literature from Oxford University, in Business Studies from Bradford University Management Centre and has a PhD from Cranfield University. He has extensive industrial experience, including a number of years as Marketing Director of Canada Dry.

During the past twenty years he has run marketing seminars and workshops in the UK, Europe, Japan, India, the Far East, Australia, South America, South Africa, Brazil and the USA.

He has written thirty books, including the best-seller *Marketing Plans: How to Prepare Them; How to Use Them*, and many of his papers have been published in a variety of journals. He is also Chairman of the Editorial Board of the *Journal of Marketing Practice: Applied Marketing Science*.

His current interests centre around the use of information technology in advanced marketing processes.

Hugh Wilson MA, DipCompSci, PhD is a Visiting Fellow at Cranfield School of Management and an independent consultant in marketing and IT.

Hugh took a mathematics degree at Oxford University and a postgraduate computer science degree at Cambridge University. He then spent ten years in the computing industry working for IBM, Logica, Artificial Intelligence Ltd and NCR in software development, consulting and marketing.

His increasing interest in marketing strategy took him to Cranfield where he undertook a major research study on IT support for marketing planning. For this research he gained a prize-winning PhD from Cranfield University. He now lectures at Cranfield on marketing planning, customer relationship management and electronic commerce.

Hugh has published several management reports and numerous papers on various topics in marketing and IT. He has carried out consultancy assignments for Hill Samuel (marketing planning), Michelin (segmentation, planning and advertising strategy), British Telecom (customer relationship management and marketing training) and Cellnet (IT-supported marketing planning), among others.

His current research interests include the efficacy of customer relationship management systems, managing the channel mix and the integration of IT and marketing strategies.

Contents

List of figures

List of tables

Cranfield School of Management Research Reports Series

The Cranfield School of Management Research Reports series is a major new initiative from Cranfield School of Management and Financial Times Prentice Hall.

The series combines the best in primary research from one of the world's foremost management schools with the traditional publishing and marketing skills of Financial Times Prentice Hall. The reports are designed to allow senior managers to apply the lessons from this research to their own organisations in order to promote best practice across a range of industries.

For further information on other titles in the series, please contact Financial Times Prentice Hall on + 44 (0) 1704 508080.

Editorial board

Dr Alan Harrison, Senior Lecturer and Exel Logistics Research Fellow, Cranfield School of Management

Gill Marshall, Corporate Communications Manager, Cranfield School of Management

Professor Malcolm McDonald, Professor of Marketing Strategy and Deputy Director, Cranfield School of Management

Dr Susan Vinnicombe, Director of Graduate Research and Reader in Organisational Behaviour, Cranfield School of Management

Professor David Tranfield, Professor of Management, Director of Research and Deputy Director, Cranfield School of Management

Professor Shaun Tyson, Professor of Human Resource Management and Head of the Strategic Human Resources Group, Cranfield School of Management

Preface

The domain of IT-enabled marketing is driven by hype and hope and there is little empirical evidence for the often wild claims made by the IT industry providers.

On the demand side, directors and managers, especially those outside the strictly functional IT domain, have grown increasingly confused by the breathtaking pace of technological progress, a progress that has theoretically made possible the transformation of marketplace to marketspace, bringing suppliers and consumers ever closer and giving those whom we serve much greater control over their own destinies.

Alas, a great divide has appeared between what is possible and what is being achieved. The time is right for someone to attempt to bring order to the confusion, some simplicity to the complexity, so that practitioners might take better advantage of the commercial possibilities made available by IT. This is what this report does. It makes the complex more understandable and provides a valuable route map through the domain.

I wish to acknowledge my great debt to Dr Hugh Wilson, who has done most of the work on this report. His vast experience and wisdom shines through every page and I thank him for his energy, drive, enthusiasm and clarity.

In the past few months, our research has also benefited considerably from our collaboration with the Information Systems Research Centre at Cranfield, and in particular the hard work and valuable insights of Professor John Ward, Frances Sutherland and Dr Liz Daniel. We are collaborating even more closely through a joint consortium-funded project which is now in progress, which aims to address some of the gaps in current knowledge which we identify in the concluding chapter.

I would also like to thank the many other busy academics and practitioners who have generously devoted time to the project.

Professor Malcolm McDonald
Cranfield School of Management

1

Introduction

1.1 INFORMATION TAILORING IN MARKETSPACE

> We are such stuff as dreams are made on.
>
> Shakespeare, *The Tempest*

The most distinctive feature of humans, although the least tangible and most mysterious, is our information processing ability. And yet it is only now that information-based products and services are accelerating past physical products as the dominant proportion of the economy. Information, increasingly encoded electronically, dominates the growth industries such as entertainment and financial services, and its electronic version of transportation is at last fighting for market share with the physical transportation that formed the great growth industry of earlier parts of the century. The century's dramatic increases in physical mobility are far from reaching a plateau – witness the continuing rise of global tourism. But the exponential increases in global communication of electronic information are sufficiently well established to justify speculation that the information revolution will be seen as a defining feature of our age.

It is widely recognised that information-based organisations are in the front line of this revolution. The Swedish Post Office is providing every Swedish citizen with an electronic mail address in an attempt to survive the decimation in paper mail that it predicts over the next decade (Acey, 1997). Book retailers face twin challenges from specialist Internet retailers and from the publishers selling directly from their own Web sites (Moody, 1997; Cope, 1999). CD retailers face the additional threat that online competitors can produce a CD tailored to the individual's tastes with the tracks they like in an order they specify (e.g. *www.musicmaker.com*), while some performers are bypassing the whole chain and downloading their music straight to the consumer (Snoddy, 1999). But however physical our needs, the information revolution is transforming industries. We need to be fed and clothed, but retailers face a major challenge from home shopping, with supermarkets moving from early prototypes through production-level trials to national rollout, and Levi's bypassing the retailers to allow direct ordering of its jeans (Robertson, 1997a, 1997b). We need to be housed, but the location of our housing in suburbs created by the physical transport revolution may be drastically modified with the increase in teleworking. We wish to stay healthy, but the health industry in which 25 per cent of costs are attributable to processing of information (Peppard, 1998) is increasingly global. A Dublin-based father used the Net to discover that King's College Hospital in London was the best place for liver transplants for babies, concluding that, 'If we hadn't used the Net, we could have had another dead baby' (Cairncross, 1997). Business-to-business sectors, led by the IT sector itself (Magretta, 1998), are facing a restructuring just as radical due to information-enabled globalisation and mass customisation.

Two great trends in information technology are supporting this revolution. The first is the coming of age of database technology. Databases have evolved as the heart of the drives over the past thirty years to increase the efficiency of supply, production, distribution and finance. The costs have often outweighed the benefits as the computing industry has passed on the costs of its painful, disaster-ridden childhood since its birth a mere forty-odd years ago. Perhaps because of this, the realisation is dawning that the more fundamental benefits of IT lie at the customer interface, through interactive exchange of information with the customer, leading to tailored, information-enhanced products offered to global niches or even markets of one. Databases that support the storage of intelligence about the customer, gathered and integrated from diverse sources, provide the engine that can realise this concept of information-based tailoring.

The second major trend in IT provides the road network, as it were, to enable the mobility of the new information-tailored products. As Adam Smith noted two centuries ago, mobility is essential if one wishes to access a large enough market to allow tailored specialisation without the cost disadvantages that caused the demise of the made-to-measure suit and, more recently, the hand-built motor-car. Computer networks have existed for decades, but rapidly decreasing telecommunication costs and gradual standardisation have supported their recent prominence through the Internet in particular.

This report, then, does not just concern the interface of two particular business functions. Although IT and marketing have been historically placed in two separate departments, both have aspirations to lie at the heart of the organisation. To quote the first of our expert respondents:

> I went to a talk shortly after the war where the chief executive of Hotpoint was talking. He said that marketing was now the central function. He said, 'We got here by making a good iron, which gets

us into the white goods business. Now it doesn't matter what we produce, or even if we produce it, as our skill is marketing.' This was not the fashion in the 1930s: everything was on the product, making it cheaply and well. Now there is no reason why one should not redraw his circle where he put marketing in the centre of the organisation, and put IT there. There is nowhere that IT does not dominate your strategy today. It used to be the airlines and the banks, and all the progammers wanted to work there because they got some kudos. It is key to get the IT strategy right in any sector. Now is that too confrontational for marketing people? I don't know.

Professor Kit Grindley

The truth is that neither function can achieve its aim of driving business strategy without the other. It is the new offering of information-tailored products to customers, through the medium of a location-independent marketspace as well as the physical marketplace, that is transforming every industry and placing IT-enabled marketing at the heart of every organisation, whether it knows it or not.

1.2 AIMS AND OVERVIEW OF METHOD

'The phonograph is of no commercial value.' Thomas Edison, 1880.
'Who the hell wants to hear actors talk?' Harry Warner, 1927.
'I think there is a world market for about five computers.' Tom Watson, Chairman, IBM, 1943.
'There is no reason for any individual to have a computer in their home.' Ken Olson, President, DEC, 1977.

Collected by Hair and Keep (1997)

Prediction is difficult in times of change. This report aims to provide an overview of IT-enabled marketing, to help organisations understand the revolution and identify how to survive it. The report is of necessity more prosaic than the subject's importance would suggest: we must break down the technologies into manageable parts and begin to delineate how they can be applied. Mapping such a large and rapidly changing domain is fraught with difficulties; we cannot hope to describe every application of IT to marketing, nor hope that our analysis will endure unchanged. But we do hope to provide a tentative map of some major features of the new and shifting terrain that at least can provide better short-term guidance than the limited perspective of a single organisation's experience.

In this attempt at a holistic view, the report draws on interviews with 12 leading industry observers and academics, listed in Appendix A, as well as an extensive literature review of current practices and other research. These interviews are complemented by eight case studies, based on face-to-face interviews with marketing, IT and general managers, which illustrate how blue-chip organisations are working towards the new information-tailored marketing, and which reveal lessons and gaps in current knowledge that are of relevance to practitioners and future researchers alike.

1.3 REPORT STRUCTURE

We have already touched on the developments in the IT industry which have provoked the current emphasis on IT at the customer interface. These developments are further examined in Chapter 2 on the drivers of change, which also looks at relevant trends in consumer behaviour and marketing, in order to show why IT-enabled marketing is so important and far-reaching.

One of the problems of a report on this field is that it is so diverse. In Chapter 3 on the e-marketing mix, we present a simple (perhaps deceptively so) 'Six "I"s' framework that encapsulates our understanding of how IT can impact the marketing function.

Many practitioners will need, though, to move beyond the clarity of vision towards which this framework aspires towards practical details of when to apply what technologies. In Chapter 4 on a map of IT in marketing, we provide a map, or architecture, of what technologies are available and discuss their current state of development.

The following two chapters take two specific parts of this map and explore them in more detail. Chapter 5 on the Internet and channel choice provides a brief review of the respects in which the Internet differs from other channels available to the marketer, and crucially when it is likely to be appropriate. Chapter 6 on software for analysis and planning compares and contrasts the different styles of IT support that are available for purposes of marketing planning and strategy formulation.

In conducting this research we found that many practitioners have passed on lessons as to what has gone right and wrong in their attempts to apply IT to marketing. In Chapter 7, Case studies, we describe some of their experiences, and illustrate many of the types of system we discuss in the report through brief descriptions of system implementation in eight organisations. By keeping these cases anonymous, we are able to report honestly about what has not worked as well as what has.

One of the aims of the study on which this report is based is to establish a future agenda for research in the field. Recommendations on where further research is required to fill gaps in current knowledge are made in Chapter 8.

2

The drivers of change

2.1 INTRODUCTION

We have mentioned the new emphasis on IT applications which deliver improved effectiveness at the customer interface. Before looking in more detail at the nature of these applications and their impact on the marketing function, we look in this chapter at the causes of this significant shift away from 'back-office' automation towards the front line of the organisation, its interaction with its customers. These causes include: developments in IT and its industry; pressures from customers which are providing a consumer pull to complement the IT industry's push; and changes in the nature and role of marketing. In doing so, we explain further two major enabling technologies that we have already mentioned: the integrated customer database and the Internet. The chapter is summarised by Figure 2.1.

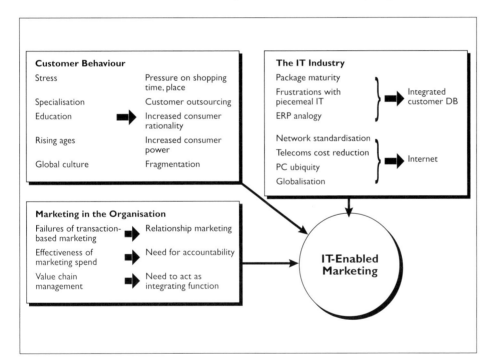

FIGURE 2.1

The drivers of change

We begin with a historical review of the past dominance of internal, efficiency-driven applications – still highly relevant for understanding how board decisions on IT investments are reached, and how the criteria for approval need to be modified to exploit the real opportunities offered by IT.

2.2 IT AND EFFICIENCY

> IT is still not thought of by general management as central to the business strategy. It is thought of as something that merely *supports* the business.
>
> Joe Peppard

Until the 1980s, it seemed that nothing could stop the forward march of the IT industry. IBM was considered the quintessential blue chip, and services companies like the UK's Logica were the darlings of government. The recession in the early 1990s contributed to a major regrouping in both the IT supplier industry and internal IT departments, as company-wide pressure on costs led to closer examination of the benefits obtained by each IT project. This was not an easy process. Not only is benefits measurement difficult:

> There has been this criticism from the top, asking what we are getting for all this money. It has led to attaching financial benefits to individual projects in a way that has never happened in other areas of the company. And I don't think it's possible, because it's an integrated effort from the whole company, albeit enabled by one or more IT projects, that delivers the benefit. The same system in two companies might have produced very different benefits. Or the benefit might simply be that we're still in business, and we've survived whereas so-and-so didn't.
>
> Professor Kit Grindley

but also, much IT spending relates to infrastructure, such as the computer networks and integrated databases that need to be in place before any specific applications are provided:

> There is still no general acceptance at board level of the need for a large spend on infrastructure, which no supplier tries to sell. What an impossible sell: 80 per cent of IT spend is on infrastructure, on which there's no benefit at all. So suppliers concentrate on 'this little box here, which will give you all these benefits'.
>
> Professor Kit Grindley

As Professor Grindley has convincingly shown (Grindley, 1995), IT staff have long counteracted these difficulties with a hidden agenda, tweaking the numbers in calculations of project return on investment in order to fit the laid-down criteria, to ensure that their favoured projects go ahead and infrastructure is developed. Why do IT professionals act so independently? One reason is to push through changes they believe to be fundamental to future business success under the more readily calculated guise of mere efficiency gains. The drawback is that without full board understanding and backing, the real benefits may not be obtained.

> I have met a number of IT directors who have a better vision for the business than the line directors. Whether they can sell it to the board is a different matter. In practice, board level involvement is rare. But it's terribly helpful when it happens.
>
> Nick Hewson

Another reason not admitted even to themselves is personal development. With high job mobility and specialised training, IT staff typically owe a greater allegiance to their profession than to the organisation employing them. If only to improve the CV, exposure to the latest technology is regarded as essential. We recall a £300 000 software project by a large, reputable computer firm which failed entirely due to the insistence of a manager on the use of the latest, sexiest software development tool, despite independent expert advice from several sources that it was utterly inappropriate to the task in hand. In this case the manager needed that updated CV as the post did not survive the project's collapse.

Economists meanwhile have taken a holistic view, finding that all the spending on computing may have increased the productivity of the office worker not one jot:

> The productivity gains of the Information Age are just a myth. There's not a shed of evidence to show that people are putting out more because of investments in technology.
>
> Stephen Roach (quoted in Griffith, 1997)

As evidence, Morgan Stanley economist Stephen Roach compares the productivity gains in the US service industry, which has received about 80–85 per cent of IT investment over the past decade, with those in US manufacturing, which has spent just 15–20 per cent of the total. While service productivity might have been expected to go up more, gains have in fact been less than 1 per cent a year, whereas the manufacturing sector has managed over 3 per cent. Roach puts what productivity gains there have been in services down to longer hours in the office – a far cry from the fears of excess leisure once computers did all the work.

Similarly, a 1997 study of UK banks found that, although they spent ten times more per employee on IT than they did in 1980, cost–income ratios had not improved at any of the big four clearing banks (Sabbagh, 1997). The report concluded that only customer inertia had saved the big banks, a factor which will not last indefinitely.

When it comes to efficiency savings, we cannot improve on the summary of William Rees-Mogg, a long-time blue-chip board member as well as an economically sophisticated journalist:

> Most senior managers now at board level have only a superficial understanding of information technology; boards are bad at deciding what they need; consultants are expensive, hard to monitor, and of variable quality; their recommendations are often inappropriate to the real needs of the business; the technology and software seldom deliver what the consultants have promised, and always cost more than the board have budgeted for; the IT systems need to be updated continuously; the once-for-all capital expenditure turns out to be an annual commitment, tending to rise year after year; the improvement in efficiency is less than has been forecast, and staff savings are much less – indeed, sometimes staff numbers actually rise; profit gains are much smaller and the IT investment is much bigger than the board had hoped for; instead of being a profitable investment, IT turns out to be a running cost.
>
> Rees-Mogg (1997)

2.3 IT AND EFFECTIVENESS

> We know what we are, but know not what we may be.
>
> Shakespeare, *Hamlet*
>
> Most marketing managers, and indeed sales directors, tend to think fairly short term. In short, they automate what they currently do.
>
> Nick Hewson

Despite the low reputation which escalating costs have bestowed on the IT professionals, there remains a widespread recognition that there is 'little choice but to continue investing, if only as a defensive response to match niche players, such as telephone banker First Direct' (Sabbagh, 1997). This example of First Direct's telephone banking service represents a comparatively modest evolution, offering the same basic transactions as a high-street bank but using the medium of the telephone and the postal service. But through the important benefit of being available 24 hours a day, with no need for the customer to visit a branch, it illustrates the crucial shift of emphasis from back-office automation to front-office added value. The realisation is dawning that while IT has a decidedly mixed record of simply improving productivity, it can enable differentiation strategies through radically different means of interacting with the customer, specifying the product and indeed in some cases delivering it.

The UK clearers, to continue with this example, don't just face the challenge of telephone banking. Niche competitors are setting up banking services on the Internet, forcing the major clearers to respond with their own Internet services (listed at *www.netbanker.com*). A North American study (Taylor, 1997), in which banks such as the Bank of Montreal have been expanding their Web services since 1995 (Foremski, 1997), calculates costs of one cent for a transaction conducted over the Net, as opposed to $1.07 for a branch transaction and 27 cents for an ATM: potential cost benefits as well as, rather than instead of, gains for the customer. Nor need these competitors be in the same country. Increasing international standardisation such as EMU is increasing the attractiveness of global investment by organisations such as AT&T which control the networks (Manchester, 1997) and the difficulties ahead for national banks. As well as basic transactions, the Internet is being used to replace human advice in product specification. Web sites such as that of Ireland's AIB can be used to work out monthly mortgage payments, relevant tax and so on using an online form into which the user enters the proposed mortgage size and payment period. New electronic intermediaries such as InsureMarket, an online site run by the computer software company Intuit, search for the best live quote from a range of life insurance companies (Denton, 1997), mimicking the services which search for the cheapest online source of a given book or CD. Online trading by private investors is surging, with a third of the $491 bn of assets managed by Charles Schwab, the largest US discount brokerage, being held in its two million online accounts (Kavanagh, 1999).

Whether viewed as an opportunity by an innovator or a problem for the late majority, IT-enabled strategies focused not on internal processes but on improving the offering to the customer are reshaping a wide range of industries. We have mentioned the two themes in IT development that are making this possible: the development of integrated customer databases and the maturing of computer networks. We will explore these in more detail before examining their impact on the nature of marketing.

2.4 THE INTEGRATED CUSTOMER DATABASE

> Sales and marketing systems are the weakest part of the mix at present, because less investment has gone in. Often you find a multiplicity of databases. Replication, duplication and inconsistency are very high. A crucial problem is the integration of information flows from the marketplace into the organisation with those into the marketplace from the organisation. This feedback loop is often not matched together. Marketing is still very push-based. Also what marketing tends to do is look for positive feedback: how many sales have we generated? But they are not getting feedback from those who haven't bought. How many people are actually being put off telecoms companies by Friends and Family schemes?
>
> Professor John Ward

> If you ask people why they are implementing sales and marketing databases, they would be very hard pressed to say anything other than 'We're collecting a load of names and addresses and trying to think afterwards what to do with it'. That's the reality a lot of the time, and it's rather pathetic. It's why these software companies are mostly so small, because few of them have figured out what the business benefits are.
>
> Professor Robert Shaw

Automation of business areas tends to follow a common pattern. Early systems are developed bespoke, written from scratch for each organisation. As the needs become better understood, suppliers look to leverage their experience by providing packaged solutions, and users seek to reduce their software development costs and risk by buying them. The market for packaged products starts with a large number of mostly small suppliers selling limited solutions which need tailoring and integration with other systems. Over time, packages increase in scope, and a shakeout occurs as the few suppliers that can afford the now considerable product development costs compete for the now substantial market.

The market for packaged customer databases or customer relationship management (CRM) systems, is following this model, and has until recently been at the intermediate stage with a multiplicity of small vendors. This stage is illustrated in the left-hand side of Figure 2.2. We can define the market roughly as systems, along with associated services, that incorporate both a customer file and also one or more of the operational areas that draw on this file to manage customer interaction. These operational areas include direct mail, telemarketing, campaign management and salesforce automation, and more recently customer interaction via the Internet. Studies in the late 1980s and early 1990s (Andersen Consulting, 1989; Shaw 1991, 1994; Hewson and Hewson, 1994) showed a market still dominated by a myriad of small suppliers. Mostly national rather than international, few had a turnover in excess of £5 million. The studies could be deceptive, in that they largely ignored the large proportion of systems that were developed bespoke either by internal IT departments or by software services companies as larger organisations found the off-the-shelf solutions inadequate for their needs. Systems often focused on one means of customer interaction, such as direct mail or salesforce automation. The small suppliers varied considerably in their ability to tackle the complex issues involved in successful implementation within the user organisation, while user companies themselves as usual tended to look for quick fixes and to underestimate the business re-engineering required. The result was high levels of customer dissatisfaction and the development of a series of piecemeal systems covering different aspects of the relationship with the customer.

FIGURE 2.2

CRM systems market: supplier size

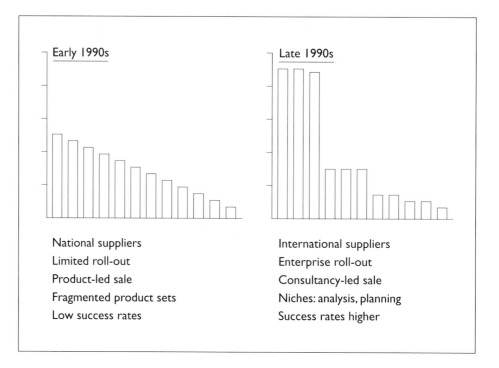

The market for customer databases is now beginning to reach the shakeout stage (illustrated on the right of Figure 2.2) as integrated, highly flexible packages are developed:

> As a change on the ground, there will be a much bigger penetration of a single piece of front-end software that is able to manage the whole of the customer interface. That is going to be very visible over the next two or three years, increasing at a compound rate. The leading vendors have 100 per cent plus growth rates.
>
> Nick Hewson

> I think there will be a big boom in this type of sales and marketing system because of big players entering with packaged software. One driver for this change is increasing internationalisation, from things like Sky television and the Web. You can't afford to have separate ways of doing things in different countries.
>
> Professor John Ward

These integrated systems potentially provide the crucial added value of integrating all the routes to the customer, whether via mail, telephone, face-to-face contact or the Internet. Hence contacts made by one route can draw on information collected by another route. This development of hybrid systems is blurring the previous division of the market between call centre systems, sales automation, direct mail and so on. The wider scope of today's systems is illustrated in Figure 2.3. Common terms used in connection with these integrated products are customer interface systems, customer asset management, customer relationship management (CRM) systems and front-office automation.

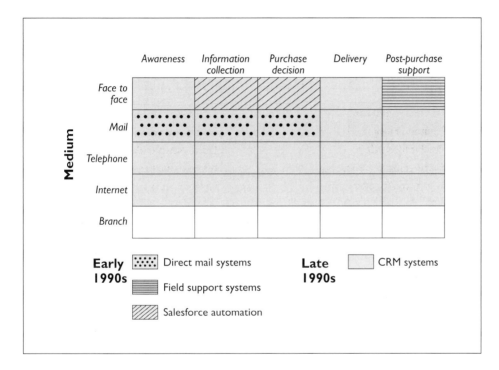

FIGURE 2.3

Integration at the customer interface

The market capitalisation of the leading vendors has grown substantially over the past two years. One of the leading vendors, Aurum, was bought in 1997 for $250 million by Baan. Other wealthy US vendors that have experienced high growth and have now established themselves in the UK include Vantive and Siebel.

This dramatic change has been influenced by the analogy with SAP, the highly successful German vendor of integrated systems for back-office automation with a turnover of over £3 bn (Lamb, 1997a; 'SAP strength rocked by low profits', *Computing*, 14 January 1999, p. 12). SAP has led the market which has become known as Enterprise Resource Planning (ERP) systems. Typically integrating finance, manufacturing logistics, distribution and human resources, these systems have become popular in large organisations, particularly manufacturing, despite the high cost and complexity of such ambitious projects, as they can in theory reduce the large costs and risks associated with integrating separate systems from separate vendors. SAP's considerable success, and the growth until recently of around 30 per cent in the ERP market as a whole (Ovum, 1997), has not been lost on software companies looking for sources of future growth:

> I think the software companies saw the analogy with SAP. SAP crept up on people. The software companies saw that there was no equivalent in sales and marketing.
>
> Professor John Ward

If the analogy was initially lost on the ERP suppliers themselves, they have wasted little time in catching up. Just as SAP's rival, Baan, as we have mentioned, purchased their way into the front office, SAP themselves have been buying into this market and rushing to improve their suite's capabilities at the customer interface, to offset their slowdown in profit growth – itself attributed to the change in fashion from back-office to front-office automation, as well as to a lull in new projects as year 2000 implementations are completed ('ERP vendors lose their Midas touch', *Computing*, 28 January 1999, p. 2).

This trend towards integrated customer-facing systems is several years behind the integration of manufacturing and accounting systems. It is interesting to note that another ERP supplier, Oracle, has been working at the component parts of its ERP solution since at least 1985. Its vast investment, initially with scant returns and numerous development problems, included the development of two parallel accounting systems over several years, one in the UK and one in the US, before standardising on one and scrapping the considerable effort in the other. But as it now reaps the rewards of this investment, it is in turn investing in front-office software to automate the customer interface. Venture capital has not been slow to follow the ERP example and provide a more rapid development path for integrated customer databases. Suppliers who already had products dealing with part of the problem, such as salesforce automation, complaint handling or field service, have also been well placed to move rapidly into the market for integrated systems by expanding their existing offerings.

2.5 WIDE AREA NETWORKS AND THE INTERNET

If integrated databases provide the means by which information is co-ordinated and distributed within the organisation, wide area networks and in particular the Internet allow this information to be electronically disseminated to customers and, in return, added to as customers interact with the organisation via electronic mail and the Web. Of course, there are plenty of other ways of interacting with customers: face to face, via paper mail, via the telephone, using media advertisements and so on. But as we shall see, electronic interaction via computer networks provides a new communication channel with quite different advantages and disadvantages from the alternatives. While by no means always appropriate for a given customer interaction, its characteristics have sufficient uses to be irrelevant to none, and for some industries a contributor to fundamental reshaping. Encyclopedia Britannica has been forced to give up its traditional face-to-face sales approach in the light of competition from Microsoft's multimedia equivalent. Dell, the PC manufacturer built on direct marketing, is now outflanking its own imitators with the added value provided by its Web site which allows the customer to configure the system interactively. The US vendors of integrated sales and marketing systems that we discussed in the last section are finally breaking down the UK market's dependence on local suppliers with the aid of richly functional Web sites used by potential customers and its own local systems integrators alike.

> The Internet is just a way of putting your e-mail address, and a site of information, onto a network across the world, using cheap communications bought off telecoms companies using leased lines. You don't need to know what it is at a technical level.
>
> Professor John Ward

The Internet is a *de facto* standard, established by market demand like Microsoft's Windows and Intel's x86 architecture, rather than by wide industry agreement like the relational database standards. As such its long-term future is difficult to predict, some believing that it will in time be replaced by other standards designed to cope with the high-volume, high-value electronic commerce with which it still struggles. But it is now clearly beyond its initial role as a powerful prototype showing the potential of standardised wide area networks in expanding interactive communication of electronic information.

Whatever the future of the Internet itself – and we shall tend to use the Internet as a shorthand for wide area networks more generally – various factors have combined to make the advent of global electronic mass communication possible. Networking technical standards have been evolving for decades, as have ideas on how to use networks for such tasks as electronic mail, discussion sites, file transfer and remote data storage and transactions. By 1985, Xerox had in place a proprietary global network in which one could print a document on a colleague's printer in another continent, browse his file server or send a document or presentation by electronic mail for comment. The use of such networks on a global, standardised scale has been aided by rapidly decreasing telecommunications costs, increasing communications bandwidth with technologies such as fibre optics, and the availability of standardised, cheap workstations in the shape of the IBM-compatible PC running Windows.

The Internet happened to be around to take advantage of this opportunity. It came into being due to a certain cold war obsession with keeping up with Russia, leading to heavy investment in connecting those quintessential knowledge organisations, the US universities and research establishments that connected to the ARPAnet, as the Internet was initially known. The World Wide Web, or Web for short, a much more recent 1990s invention, is technically just one Internet application which allows organisations to provide a number of pages of information on a 'Web site', which can be browsed by interested parties. It derives its name from the ability to embed 'hypertext links' in each page, which connect the pages in a web of links. Clicking on a highlighted piece of text – 'R/3', for example, on SAP's Web site – might lead to a description of its R/3 product on a separate page. These links may be to pages on a Web site belonging to a totally different organisation, such as a reference to an Oracle database which can be used to underlie SAP's R/3 product.

This concept of hypertext, as the resulting combination of text and links to related text is named, has again been in existence for some considerable time (for a pre-Web review see Wilson, 1990), but is now proving its importance in enabling the user to 'navigate', or find his/her way round, large quantities of information. The idea for hypertext originated with Vannevar Bush, the senior US scientist during the Second World War (Nyce and Kahn, 1992). Starting from the premise that a library should be a memory machine, Bush wished to mimic the brain's associative memory. He therefore described a hypothetical machine named Memex, a personal memory assistant managing a library of microfilm, which would allow the user to specify that two microfilm frames should be linked together. If you spotted an interesting connection between two ideas – say, this section and your current project to develop a sales brochure for a new range of widgets – you could make a link between them. Next time you looked at the brochure draft, you would be reminded of the link which would enable you to find this section easily, prompting you to consider providing a Web version of the brochure with hypertext links for easier navigation. Although conceived as an analogue machine, the concept has inspired digital software designers of several generations (including one of the authors, as illustrated in Wilson, 1989). The implementation of the concept that forms the Web has proved one of the major drivers of the Internet's explosive growth.

2.6 CHANGES IN CONSUMER BEHAVIOUR AND MARKETING

If the Internet and integrated customer databases are enabling closer interaction with the customer, the function that has traditionally been responsible for the customer interface – marketing – has had its own reasons for moving in the same direction.

- *The failures of transaction-based marketing.* The growing recognition of the importance of customer retention (Reichheld and Sasser, 1990) has clarified the dangers of viewing each sale as a separate event. Hence there are widespread attempts to implement 'relationship marketing', concerned with 'the establishment of enduring and mutually profitable relationships between the firm and its customers' – attempts which point up the importance of integrated, detailed information about each customer.

- *The pressure on marketing spend.* As the very existence of a separate marketing department became questioned in the early 1990s recession (Brady and Davis 1993), marketing staff came under increasing pressure to justify expenditure. This has increased the attractiveness of the IT-supported 'addressable' media such as direct mail and the telephone for reaching the customer, as compared to mass media where effectiveness may be more difficult to measure.

- *Value chain management.* Whether under the label of value chain management, business process redesign or total quality, organisations are increasingly thinking across departmental boundaries in order to concentrate on adding value for the customer. Marketing has been shamed that these initiatives have mainly originated elsewhere – in manufacturing, in the IT department, or from consultants brought in to manage a crisis. The need for marketing to act as an integrating function in co-ordinating the organisation's interaction with the customer, always present in the textbooks, is now more widely recognised, and even in some cases practised. But attempts to enforce procedures representing marketing best practice with paper can easily be undercut by departments without a strong self-interest to comply – witness the sorry failure of many attempts to institute company-wide planning procedures, where the vital issue of 'buy-in' is often ignored. IT offers marketing staff the opportunity to embed their notions of best practice into the organisation:

> IT can embed discipline because when a computer tells you to do something, you can't really avoid doing it. It's difficult for centralised marketing to impose an infrastructure. Certain things can be centralised, like branding, and marketing strategy. But attempts to impose procedures can easily be ignored: it's easy for human beings to duck and weave. In the days when you could shoot people for disobedience it was different.
>
> Professor Kit Grindley

- *Trends in customer behaviour.* Marketing has also been subject to consumer pull. Today's first-world consumers are more highly educated, under higher stress, more specialised, living longer and more influenced by global culture than those of the 1960s and 1970s when our view of marketing was formed. This is resulting (Sheth and Sisodia, 1997) in various changes to consumer behaviour, such as: an increased pressure on shopping time; a trend towards outsourcing by consumers, such as the increase in ready meals; increased consumer rationality; a fragmentation of consumer markets; and, overall, an increase in the consumer's power relative to the producer's. Nor are these trends specific to consumers. As McDonald, Denison and Ryals (1994) found, customer expertise, sophistication and power are increasing likewise in industrial goods and services markets. This power shift stems partly from the concentration of buying into fewer hands, evident in many industries, and partly from the development of buyer groups, networks and alliances, all recent phenomena which have swung market control away from manufacturers. These trends in customer behaviour collectively put considerable demands on the organisation's information systems.

2.7 SUMMARY

We have explored the shift of focus away from automation of the company's internal operations towards applications that enable new ways of interacting with customers. To be sure, the reasons for this shift include a great deal of technology push from the computing industry, looking to sustain its growth, but we have also explored how applications which add value for the customer are ultimately of considerably more importance than efficiency-driven IT which struggles to provide the intended cost savings.

We have discussed two important technical trends underlying this shift: integrated customer databases and the Internet. In due course we will provide further detail on these and other relevant technologies. But first we need a bridge between the concept of added value at the customer interface and the morass of technical detail. We endeavour to provide this bridge in the next chapter, which offers an overview of what IT can do for the marketer.

3

The e-marketing mix

We have examined some of the trends in IT and in marketing that are allowing their current powerful combination. In this chapter we present a simple 'six "I"s' framework that summarises how IT can impact the marketing function, and that hence provides a basis for identifying opportunities and predicting future changes. These six 'I's show the levers, as it were, that are available for the marketing manager to pull through the use of IT. Like marketing's four 'P's, it does not follow that each of these levers must be pulled fully in every situation. In the same way that not every product requires a low price, it is clear that not every product requires information-enabled individualisation, for example. These choices must depend, as always, on the needs of specific customer segments and their matching to the organisation's capabilities and desires. But a starting-point is to be clear on what options are available. The framework is summarised in Figure 3.1.

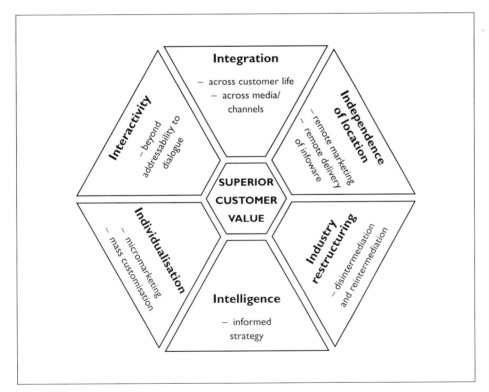

FIGURE 3.1

The dimensions of IT-enabled marketing

3.1 INTEGRATION: KNOW YOUR CUSTOMER

The need for management of customer relationships implies the need for systems which manage data on the whole of the customer interaction, throughout the customer lifecycle, from initial contact, through configuration and sales, to delivery and post-sales service. The multiple channels by which the consumer demands to be able to reach the supplier imply that these data must also be integrated across communication mechanisms, so a telephone operator will know about a letter that was sent yesterday, and Pfizer field sales representatives can call on information about orders placed by phone, or review market data refreshed daily from US Pharmaceuticals Group databases (Dragoon, 1995). Another example of integration through the customer lifecycle, which illustrates how data integration can enforce best practice, was provided some time ago by Rover:

> Rover designed a system for their dealers where the customer could walk through the motor-car on the screen just as one would walk through a kitchen. Having designed the car on the system, and determined the delivery date and so on, that would become EDI instructions to the various suppliers and contractors. Even the maintenance was dealt with subsequently through the same system, so the history of the car was available online. Now you could call that groupware. It gives the dealer interaction the whole time about how to handle the sale. If he doesn't follow the procedure, there's an electronic supervisor that ensures he conforms. Now that ensures that the marketing strategy is followed. That's quite a new idea. It's best marketing practice built into the IT.
>
> Professor Kit Grindley

3.2 INTERACTIVITY: BEYOND ADDRESSABILITY TO DIALOGUE

Knowing your customers means closing the loop between the messages sent to them and the messages they send back. IT is supporting an increased use of interactive communication mechanisms, such as telephone and the Internet, to complement less interactive mechanisms such as mail or mass media advertisements. It has been said that this is the 'age of addressability' as organisations have endeavoured to communicate with individual customers through direct mail (Blattberg and Deighton, 1991). Interactivity goes one step further, supporting a dialogue rather than a one-way communication – although there will of course continue to be many occasions when the asynchronous interactivity of the reply coupon is sufficient and appropriate.

Whatever the mechanisms used, interactive communication is essential if the aims of relationship marketing – a long-term relationship with customers, in which continually refreshed customer knowledge is used to ensure that their needs are met, leading to customer satisfaction, higher retention rates and enhanced lifetime customer value – are to be realised. The IT systems that underpin this relationship need to be accompanied, though, by a substantial shift in thinking about the nature of the sales process and corresponding changes to internal processes, as illustrated in Figure 3.2.

FIGURE 3.2

An interaction view of the sales process

Supplier perspective		Interaction perspective		Buyer perspective	
Advertising	Selling	Marketing activity	Interaction	Decision theory	Consumer behaviour
Brand awareness		Define markets/ understand value Create value proposition	*Recognise exchange potential*	Problem recognition	Category need
	Prospecting		*Initiate dialogue*		Awareness
Brand attitude – info re benefits – brand image – feelings – peer influence	Provide information		*Exchange information*	Information search	Attitude Information gathering and judgement
Trial inducement	Persuade		*Negotiate/tailor*	Evaluation of alternatives	
	Close sale		*Commit*	Choice/purchase	Purchase process
	Deliver		*Exchange of value*		
Reduce cognitive dissonance	Service		*Monitor*	Post-purchase behaviour	Post-purchase experience

Traditional models of advertising and sales, on the left of the figure, are based on a 'push' model of marketing in which, after the product is made, prospects are found and persuaded to buy the product. The delivery and service that follow are operational functions with little relationship to marketing.

Traditional models of buyer behaviour, illustrated on the right of the figure, assume more rationality on the part of buyers but underplay the importance of what the buyer says back to the seller. The seller's offering is assumed to be predetermined rather than developed in conjunction with the buyer.

The interaction perspective in the middle column provides a new breakdown of the sales process (in italics). Rather than 'problem recognition' on the part of the buyer, we label this stage *recognise exchange potential* – a mutual recognition of the potential for an exchange of value which is beneficial to both parties. Rather than prospecting, we use the term *initiate dialogue* to emphasise that the dialogue may be initiated by either party. Rather than just the seller providing information, the parties *exchange information* about the buyer's needs as well as the seller's offerings. Persuasion may be involved, but more generally the parties *negotiate and tailor* what will be provided by the seller, and what value (typically though not exclusively monetary) the buyer will provide in return. Closing the sale is better viewed as a *commit* step from both parties. The post-sales service is really a crucial part of the *exchange of value* which takes place, as the service surround becomes increasingly important in differentiating similar basic products. Finally, both parties will wish to *monitor* the value they have given and what they have received.

These distinctions are not just playing with words. Marketing managers at one company recently relayed to us their early experience with a Web site which was enabling them to reach new customers considerably more cost-effectively than their traditional salesforce. When the Web site was first launched, potential customers were finding the company on the Web, deciding the products were appropriate on the basis of the Web site, and sending an e-mail to ask to buy. So far so good. But stuck in a traditional model of the sales process, the company would allocate the 'lead' to a salesperson, who would telephone and make an appointment perhaps three weeks hence. The customer would by now probably have moved on to another online supplier who could sell the product today, but those that remained were subjected to a sales pitch that was totally unnecessary, the customer having already decided to buy. Those that were not put off would proceed to be registered as able to buy over the Web, but the company had lost the opportunity to improve its margins by using the salesforce more judiciously. In time the company realised its mistake: unlike those prospects that the company identified and contacted, which might indeed need 'selling' to, many new Web customers were initiating the dialogue themselves, and simply required the company to respond effectively and rapidly. The salesforce were increasingly freed up to concentrate on major clients and on relationship building.

The use of interactive media is also of little use if the data thus collected are not integrated in order to build a view of the customers and their requirements over time. The example in Figures 3.3 and 3.4 illustrates a move towards greater interactivity and integration in a company that maintains consumer products on behalf of consumers and, in some cases, corporate customers. It is instructive in that the changes made are incremental, moving from a situation that is not wholly wrong to one that is not wholly right, under the constraints of the complexities of IT development and the vast investment already made in 'legacy' systems.

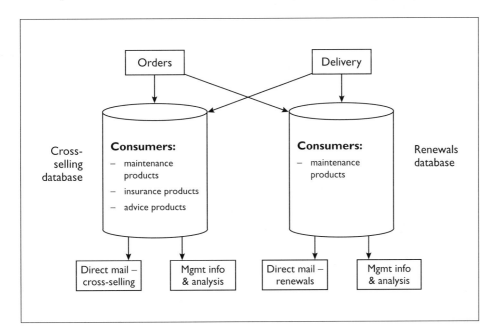

FIGURE 3.3

A consumer product maintenance company – current situation

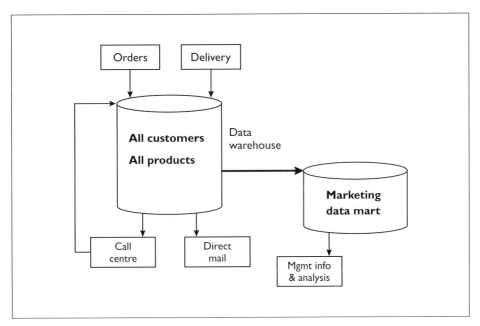

FIGURE 3.4

A consumer product maintenance company – planned situation

At present, the core maintenance services have their own renewals database designed to increase the customer retention rate. A cross-selling database uses much of the same information in order to generate business for related products such as insurance and advice services. Both databases are updated from the same operational systems dealing with order handling and delivery of the maintenance product through a field engineer force.

One problem with this situation is that the two activities are not co-ordinated: a customer may receive a renewal mailing just before a cross-selling mailing, and may object that his or her response to the first was not taken into account in the second. The data from the different systems can be difficult to analyse: names and addresses, for example, are duplicated, sometimes with minor differences, so it is difficult to establish a complete view of the customer. And separate systems support the corporate customers, so analysis by product type is difficult.

As shown in Figure 3.4, the company is replacing the two marketing databases with an integrated data warehouse, which holds information about all customers and all products. Copies of parts of these data, kept carefully synchronised, will be used for purposes such as a marketing data mart for marketing information and analysis, and an operational system for call centre support. If all goes to plan, now a single mailing could encourage the customer to renew based on a bundled package with other related services, assessed according to all available information about the customer's needs, and priced according to an assessment of the customer's overall value. A call centre with access to the same information widens the marketing options available to the company.

3.3 INDIVIDUALISATION: INFORMATION-ENABLED TAILORING

This product maintenance company also illustrates the opportunity to individualise the service provided, once integrated information about the customer is available. Tesco now produce different versions of their loyalty-card magazine based on the customer's interests. Online newspapers can be tailored to provide the topics buyers want. Other examples are provided by data warehousing expert Sean Kelly:

> I think the world is going through a phenomenal change in business culture. Every customer wants to be treated differently. My wife is phenomenally loyal to a store in Dublin which has loyalty cards, which stocks things that she likes to buy. So she knows that her favourite Italian wine will be in stock, and her shopping can be pre-packed for her, so a shop that used to take an hour now takes ten minutes. Or I buy all my business books now from a bookstore that's

based in Phoenix, Arizona. Why? Because they analyse what I buy, and every time there's a new book on data warehouses they e-mail me saying, 'Dear Mr Kelly, From your patterns you seem to be interested in data warehouses. There are these two new books published in the last month: would you be interested?' I don't have time to wander around Foyles every month. Consumers are just not going to tolerate mass production organisations.

Sean Kelly

The heavily IT-enabled direct sales approach of Dell is interesting in many ways, of which one is its individualisation of the product, the price and surrounding services. Dell's channel structure is summarised in Figure 3.5.

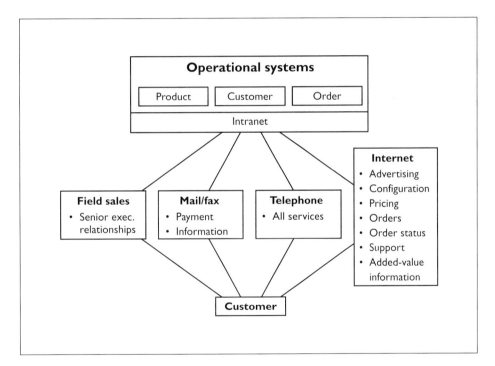

FIGURE 3.5

Dell: channel structure

Dell began by selling personal computers 'off the page' in the computer press, using mail and the telephone to undercut dramatically its rivals with their expensive networks of field salesforces and shops – though it has since added a small field salesforce to concentrate on senior relationships within its largest clients. Its experience in telephone selling gave it a natural head start in understanding how the Internet could be effectively added to the channel mix: indeed, the manager responsible for its Web site has claimed that, 'If a company does not know anything about telemarketing, it must learn about it before developing an Internet strategy' (Hill, 1997). For example, it had been forced from an early stage to collect and distribute integrated information about its customers and their purchases, so that any telephone operator could deal effectively with any call. When a Web site was added as an alternative route to purchase, it was linked into the same databases so it could share the same information on products, customers and orders – unlike many early experimenters with the Internet, who have contented themselves with a disconnected department on the side of the organisation with few attempts to tailor the service provided to each customer, or even to find out who they are.

Dell's Web site provides all the same services that are available by telephone, plus some more. In addition to the usual 'brochure-ware' of words and pictures describing what products are available, the site includes:

- a configuration service that helps the user to tailor the computer they want, and calculates its price;

- a facility to order online – alternatively, the user can print out details and order by other means such as fax, post or telephone;

- information on the order's status, lead time and so on;

- automated customised pricing for its major 'platinum' customers;

- added-value services such as online support, information on future product releases and discussion forums for users to communicate with each other.

The high proportion of visitors to the site who ultimately place their order by other mechanisms such as the telephone is an important point which emphasises that the impact of the Internet cannot be measured simply by measuring online sales, and more generally that IT-enabled channels are often complementary:

> We don't see Dell.com as a competing channel. We see it as a complementary channel. A lot of people visit Dell.com and then call us on the telephone and buy. Is that a bad thing? No, because it takes six to eight telephone calls to sell a computer, and we just made five of them go away, with a commensurate reduction in operating expenses.
>
> (Hill, 1997)

3.4 INDEPENDENCE OF LOCATION: THE DEATH OF DISTANCE

What is the difference between shoes made to measure by the village cobbler and a kitchen made to order by an Internet design service? Both achieve individualisation, but the latter combines it with post-industrial revolution economies of scale. It is able to do this because the design service can serve a widely spread geographical population, using the data transport provided by the Internet and the physical transport of our late twentieth-century infrastructure, plus a database-driven manufacturing facility. Independence of location allows individualisation to be achieved economically. Niche products can serve their target markets even if spread globally.

Being able to reach your customers wherever they are can also widen consumer choice and extend consumer power. As we have mentioned, software 'agents' are now available that will search the Web for the online bookstore that stocks a particular book at the lowest price, hence outsourcing a time-consuming activity while tending to level prices (as tends to happen in a given geographical location due to local competition). Interestingly, however, prices are not always lowered by this consumer power: a study of Japanese online car auctions (Lee, 1998) found that online prices were in this case higher, as sellers were able to reach a larger potential audience in the search for a buyer prepared to pay a given price.

The impact that independence of location can have on market structure is clearly illustrated by the increasing importance of the Internet in sales of books, pre-recorded music and videos, particularly so far in the US (Figure 3.6). The traditional market structure is dominated by local bookshops and other retail outlets. Telephone sales have had a relatively minor impact as the customer needs to know exactly what item is required without further browsing. Mail order has carved out a number of niches, in which a limited catalogue sent by post has been sufficient to meet the browsing needs of, say, science fiction enthusiasts or keen gardeners. But Internet booksellers such as Amazon are proving a much more successful challenge to the local bookshop. Large catalogues can be provided online without the prohibitive expense of printing and mailing, while browsing can be enhanced by computer search facilities. The added value is accompanied by lower costs: low unit cost transactions with a computer replace the high cost of shop assistants, and capital does not need to be tied up in moving books into expensive retail space. Naturally the retailers are fighting back with their own Web sites, and some publishers are bypassing both with their own Web sites, but the principle is clear that, at least for many purchases, a direct purchase provides greater value and convenience to the customer at lower cost, and hence with lower prices. A challenge to printed books can also be anticipated from electronic publishing, whereby the product is distributed electronically, not just ordered electronically. Similarly, the direct distribution of music over the Internet, paid for by track at very low prices, is severely worrying the major record labels which have so far remained committed to the physical CD.

FIGURE 3.6

Independence of location: the book market

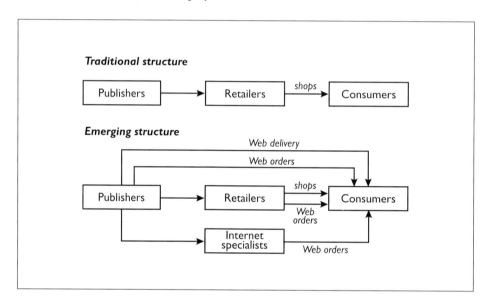

3.5 INTELLIGENCE: INFORMED STRATEGY

Better customer data can also improve decisions on marketing strategy. When a major computer manufacturer discovered that it could not measure its market share of particular application areas such as accounting, personnel and stock control, it changed its order procedures to track the type of use to which the computer was being put on purchase. This information could then be aggregated to enable effective planning, as well as enabling initiatives to serve particular segments more effectively. In this example of the use of customer information to provide intelligence for decision making, the segments were pre-determined. But in some cases, the segmentation itself is being derived from the data that have been gathered. A classic example of 'mining' information to find nuggets of value is described by Sean Kelly (using the American 'diapers' for the English 'nappies'):

The great example was Wal-Mart, where the data mining tool discovered a connection between the sale of beer and the sales of diapers, which was completely counter-intuitive. They discovered that about 2 per cent of weekday sales were from men who come in and just buy beer and diapers. Of course, what was going on was that men who didn't normally shop would be asked by their wife to pop in and buy some diapers, and while they were about it they would buy some beer. So Wal-Mart put beer on display next to the diapers, which they would never normally have done, and claimed a 10 million dollar benefit. Nobody would ever have had a hypothesis about this. So data mining tools discover hot spots in the data, that all those with blond hair and blue eyes in Huddersfield buy hot dogs on the night of the full moon, and then you can ask why on earth that happens.

Sean Kelly

Another unexpected relationship was that between chain saw and bed sales in Minnesota in October. It turned out to be due to people getting holiday homes ready for the hunting season (Freeman, 1997).

Another example of the generation of intelligence to inform marketing strategy is causal modelling – one of the many types of analysis which is finding itself labelled under the 'data mining' heading that is currently in vogue. As illustrated in Figure 3.7 (based on a real case but with invented numbers), causal modelling is a technique which investigates the connection between various 'cause' or 'independent' variables – such as price, level of promotion and advertising spend – and an 'effect' or 'dependent' variable – in this case, the size of a market. All other things being equal, total market sales of, say, beef will go up in various circumstances: when the price goes down; when the producers advertise more heavily; and when there are fewer health scares (in this case measured by the number of press releases relating to BSE from the relevant ministry). Through the statistical technique of multiple regression (or various alternatives such as neural net algorithms), the relative importance of the 'cause' variables can be established by examining data from the past (illustrated by six rows in the figure, though in practice many more are required). This means that if the marketer can predict the future value of the 'cause' variables, the computer can predict the corresponding value of the 'output' variable. So the effect on sales of, say, a price war or a future health scare can be anticipated. We look at the uses and abuses of this technique in Chapter 6, and in cases F and G in Chapter 7.

FIGURE 3.7

**Generating market
knowledge: causal modelling
in meat products company**

	Price	Promotion	Advertising	Consumer spending	BSE index	Market sales
Jan 95	2.11	10	45.1	121	12	1154
Jul 95	2.21	5	40.9	127	11	1213
Jan 96	1.97	15	35.1	131	35	950
Jul 96	1.80	20	50.4	133	32	920
Jan 97	2.05	15	48.3	137	12	1101
Jul 97	2.10	10	35.1	141	14	1081

- If prices drop by 10% market sales will increase by 7%
- If a serious BSE scare occurs, sales will drop by 23%

3.6 INDUSTRY RESTRUCTURING: REDRAWING THE MARKET MAP

If our previous 'I's can be regarded as opportunities to change our marketing approach through use of IT, this final category represents the observation that if we do not exploit these opportunities, someone else will. Viewed from outside the industry, the net effect of IT-enabled marketing will often be radical industry transformation. As we have seen from the book example, some industries are already being restructured as organisations redefine themselves to take advantage of IT-enabled marketing or are replaced by newcomers who operate according to the new rules. This is a 'third-order effect' in Joe Peppard's classification of the impacts of IT on industry structures:

The first-order effect is a partial substitution of human co-ordination by IT. For example, the first-order data processing systems replaced some clerical jobs. In terms of a transport analogy, first-order transport of bicycles simply replaces walking by cycling the same journey. The second-order effect is of increased co-ordination. Just as in travel, people travelled more, with IT a travel agent can search for more flight options using a computer reservation system. A third-order effect is a shift towards more co-ordination-intensive structures, a virtual organisation being an example of that. This is analogous to the introduction of suburbs and satellite towns as a structure that is affected by the greater transport capability. Nike is an example of a reconfigured organisation. They don't do any purchasing or manufacturing. All they do is design and market. Manufacturing, distribution and sales are all outsourced. Benetton is the original virtual organisation, using independent designers, independent agents, 700 small manufacturers, no distribution. So they become the owners of the business concept and the coordinators. Now this isn't possible without the increased co-ordination capabilities of IT. Research has shown the average firm size to be getting smaller: one of the reasons might be the move towards the virtual organisation.

Joe Peppard

An information-intensive industry in which restructuring is already well under way is that of retail financial services. The traditional model of local banks (as well as local insurance offices and building society branches), illustrated by Figure 3.8, is based on information-processing needs: the need for pieces of paper to document transactions and to represent money; the need for a person to conduct a routine transaction (bank clerks) or to provide face-to-face advice (bank managers). The bank may outsource the origination of some products, such as investment products or mortgages, but it aims to act as a unified distribution channel for a wide range of products to the consumer.

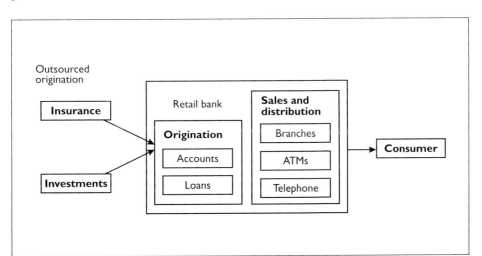

FIGURE 3.8

Retail banking: one-stop-shop model

This model has been under threat for some time, and will change further (Evans and Wurster, 1997), perhaps along the lines of the speculative Figure 3.9. Telephone banking in the style of First Direct is a first step, involving the replacement of the local branch by the telephone for some transactions, but preserving the principle that a single 'bank' can provide a range of products. At first sight the Internet banking which UK banks are currently rolling out is similar. But new intermediaries are appearing, for example the personal financial management programs such as Quicken, which help the user to keep track of their money. Many US users access their banks via software links to their financial management packages. But they are proving more loyal to their software packages than to their banks – a finding important for the power of the software provider. Other intermediaries that are making it more difficult for the banks to keep their 'one-stop-shop' role include agents such as *www.rate.com*, which searches for the best finance rates, and *www.iii.co.uk*, which will help investors to manage their portfolios.

FIGURE 3.9

Retail banking: disintermediation and reintermediation

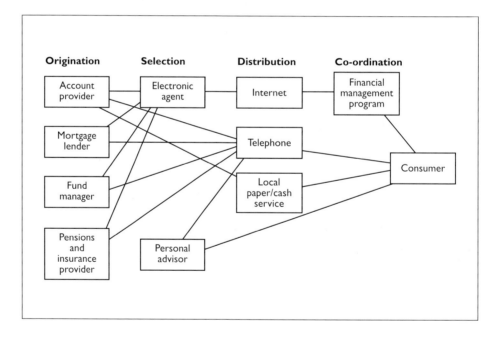

Naturally this information-intensive industry is under particularly radical change. But every industry has a substantial information-processing component in the interaction with the customer. The changes we have described in such relatively physical industries as bookselling and sales of computers illustrate that no one can afford to ignore the potential impact on their industry of IT-enabled customer communications.

4

A map of IT
in marketing

4.1 INTRODUCTION

The last chapter provided an overview of the strategic impact of IT on marketing. Many practitioners will need, though, to move beyond this towards practical details of when to apply what technologies. In this chapter we provide a map, or architecture, of what technologies are available, and discuss their current state of development.

The map is summarised by Figure 4.1, which shows the most common data held and manipulated by the marketing function, and some of the most common functions which use these data. A single IT system will support a subset of the data and a subset of the functions. For example, products described as 'marketing databases' or 'customer interface systems' typically support one or more of the sales management, direct mailing, telemarketing and electronic marketing functions. Arrows are used to indicate data flow.

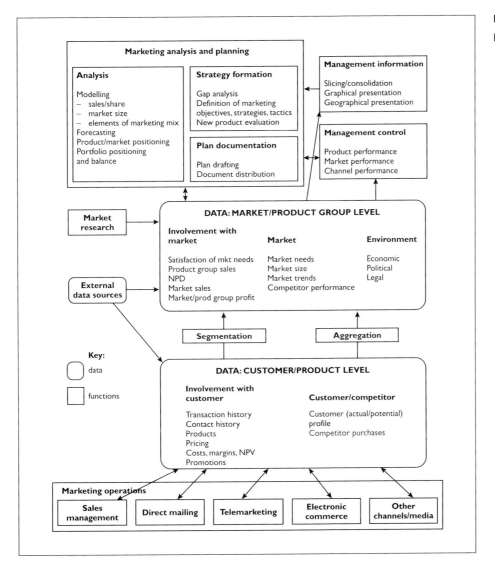

FIGURE 4.1

Information use in marketing

Marketing data can be broadly divided into two: operational data that deal with individual products, customers and transactions; and aggregated data where the unit of analysis is the market segment, market or product group.

4.2 OPERATIONAL DATA: CUSTOMERS, PRODUCTS AND TRANSACTIONS

At the level of individual customers and products, a variety of data may be held on actual and potential customers. Holding some degree of customer information is often taken as the minimal requirement of a marketing database. The information can range from basic reference data such as name, address and postcode to demographic data such as age, sex and income, and psychographic data on attitudes and lifestyle collected from surveys (Fletcher, 1995). In industrial markets, information may be richer and more detailed about a smaller number of customers, covering for example organisational structure, key contacts and their roles, the customer's value chain and so on. As well as details of customers' purchases from the organisation (discussed below), information may be held on their purchases from competitors. Information may relate to both direct and indirect customers, though typically it is weaker for the latter, and a similar range of information may be held for distributors and other relevant bodies or individuals such as influencers and sources of referrals. In the paper market described in case A, for example, graphic designers form an important influencer about whom information is collected (*see* section 7.2).

Information on the customer's involvement with the organisation is also typically held in marketing databases. Transaction data can include items such as what products have been purchased at what price, the buying channel used, purchasing frequency and account balance. The transaction data typically reference product data, which include product codes, pricing and in some cases information on costs, margins and promotions. Contact history information, such as sales contacts, mailings, complaints, service calls and proposals, may also be held. This may include soft data on why the customer did or did not buy, aiding analysis of market needs and the extent to which the organisation is satisfying them at the aggregated, market level.

This information may be held in a separate marketing database, or it may be integrated into the organisation's operational systems. Stand-alone marketing databases may have links to operational systems such as sales order processing, stock control and sales ledger, though a surprisingly high proportion have historically not made them (Hewson and Hewson, 1994).

4.3 OPERATIONAL FUNCTIONS: THE CUSTOMER INTERFACE

Drawing on these operational data, most 'customer interface' products and many bespoke systems provide functions to support one or more of the channels to the customer:

- *Salesforce automation.* This can include salesforce productivity tools such as contact management, order entry, checking inventory and order status, diary management and reporting of expenses. Often now involving notebook computers used by the salesforce in the field, the key facility is 'contact management', making all aspects of the contact with the customer available to the salesperson: notes of previous meetings, records of orders placed, notes on service issues and complaints and so on (Semanoff, 1996). Integration with the Internet can include querying online databases to generate leads or find more information about a prospect, the Maximizer product, for example, allowing the Eagle online database of North American businesses to be searched by contact name, title and so on (Datamation, 1997), as well as e-mail for the salesforce to communicate with each other and with back-office staff. Benefits can include elimination of mistakes in pricing and configuration (Blodgett, 1997), and better inventory control. Features can also include management functions such as automated reports on staff performance, sales activity, forecasts versus actuals and so on.

- *Direct mailing.* Systems supporting direct mailing provide functions such as selecting a subset of a mailing list, customising letters and address labels, selecting appropriate literature, and tracking and forwarding leads (Peacock, 1998; Moriarty and Swartz, 1989). Management of lists can include facilities such as de-duplication, where two or more lists have been combined, and data quality reporting.

- *Telemarketing.* This typically includes management of call lists, scripting of the dialogue with the prospect, and tracking and forwarding leads for order entry (Vernon, 1999). Again, data management of lists can form a major part of the system.

- Electronic commerce: Electronic links between the organisation's computers and those of the customer provide an alternative channel for advertising, prospecting, sales and post-sales support, as well as for product/service delivery in some cases. These links may be implemented using the Internet, or using other wide area networks such as those developed for electronic data interchange in cases such as the automotive industry.

Whatever the route to the customer, there is also a need for *campaign management*. Systems that support one or more of the above channels to the customer may support all steps of a campaign, from definition of objectives to recording and analysing campaign results.

For some examples of use of the customer database, *see* cases A, B and C in Chapter 7.

4.4 AGGREGATED DATA: MARKETS AND PRODUCT GROUPS

The transaction-level data can be aggregated into data at the level of markets or market segments, and product groups or product-market combinations. This provides information at a sufficiently summarised level for marketing management analysis, planning and control. The data can broadly be regarded as falling into the categories of market information, information about the company's involvement in the market, and the wider economic, political or legal environment.

4.5 MARKET RESEARCH AND OTHER EXTERNAL DATA SOURCES

Some data at this aggregated level may be imported from outside the organisation, such as from market research (e.g. customer needs, customer product perceptions, relative market shares) and from external databases (e.g. market sizes, other market information). For consumer markets, a wealth of information on UK individuals can now be purchased from standard databases. The major types of information available are:

- *Geodemographic information.* Derived largely from census data, geodemographic information is so called because it combines geographical information on where a household is located with demographic information on the age, education, family composition, income and so on of the residents. The census data themselves are at the level of enumeration districts of about 200 households, which can be complemented by individual electoral roll data. The raw data can be analysed directly if the skills are available, but for many purposes, a standard classification such as ACORN is often used. CACI's ACORN, 'A classification of residential neighbourhoods', divides the UK into 17 major groups of neighbourhoods, such as 'wealthy achievers, suburban areas' and 'council estate residents, high unemployment', each of which can be further subdivided (O'Connor and Galvin, 1997). Another such database is CCN's Mosaic, which illustrates the increasingly complex combination of data sources combined by the information providers in that it includes financial information gained from CCN's major business as a credit referencing agency.

- *Lifestyle information.* The household surveys that request information on what the household purchases in exchange for coupons have now reached a high proportion of households. The merging of two major players, CMT and NDL, allowed the launch of Claritas' Lifestyle Census product in 1995, which includes data on an impressive 75 per cent of UK households. In Claritas' Universe database, launched in late 1997, data have now been guessed, or 'modelled', for the remaining 25 per cent, based on a variety of sources such as the electoral roll, share registers, County Court judgements, and NDL's ANNA system, which guesses a person's age based on their first name – girls called Agnes or Ethel being unusual in recent decades (Sleight, 1997). Data can also be guessed based on data from neighbouring houses with the same postcode (Claritas' PAD, or Postcode Aggregated Data file).

- *Industrial markets.* Companies House is the main source of data on industrial firms. Private agencies offer alternative sources, sometimes with added details on job titles, department sizes and so on.

Data obtained externally may be used as they stand, to form a prospect list, for example, or they may be integrated with internal information. Since 1986 it has been possible to apply a neighbourhood classification code to customer data using Mosaic (Daisley, 1997).

4.6 SEGMENTATION AND AGGREGATION

The process of segmentation is rarely straightforward. It is not too difficult to assess whether a segmentation, once proposed, is a good one: the segments will be of adequate size, members will be similar to each other but different from other segments, the segments will be reachable, and the criteria for describing the segments will be relevant to the purchase situation. But there are many possible variables to use in order to divide the potential market into these segments – demographic, geographic, psychographic (relating to attitudes, lifestyle and personality) and behavioural (relating to usage rate, loyalty, purchase patterns, etc.). Which variables will result in the most powerful segmentation is a major issue, but not fundamentally an IT one. IT is, however, relevant in supplying the raw information and providing analysis tools.

Data sources

Internal systems mainly hold basic geographic and demographic data. The storage of behavioural data on the customers' past usage is increasing as loyalty cards and electronic point-of-sale systems provide more raw information, and data warehouses allow large files of past behaviour to be economically stored. The main disadvantage of segmenting on the basis of internal data, though, is that information is typically only available on current customers (and possibly lapsed ones and current prospects). Hence the external data sources discussed in the previous section are often relevant. The uses and limitations of internal data for segmentation are summarised in Figure 4.2.

FIGURE 4.2

Customer databases in segmentation

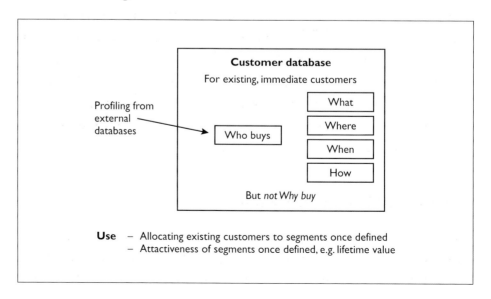

Profiling

Profiling is one means of combining these internal and external data for which IT support is available. Profiling involves seeing what the customers in the selected segments have in common, typically based on internal data, and using these criteria to select likely candidates from wider lists. One can analyse, for example, the characteristics of customers who respond well to particular marketing tools or who are loyal and profitable. The Scottish blood transfusion service, for example, used CACI software to analyse who has the greatest propensity to give blood, resulting in two segments – one affluent group with high educational qualifications and professional or managerial jobs, and another less well-off group who are public spirited, live close to town centres and probably live alone (Marsh, 1996). This information was used to seek new donors who fell into these segments.

Cluster analysis

IT support is also available to analyse market research data. Cluster analysis, for example, can group the respondents into segments relevant to their purchase decisions. An exhaust company researched consumer attitudes towards different fitters such as KwikFit and found that consumers could be divided into a few segments: one buying mainly on price, one segment of technical consumers who made their own assessment of the technical merits of the options, and one heavily influenced by brand advertising and the local fitter. This particular company was doing well with the technical segment, but not so well with brand-influenced consumers, with clear implications for marketing strategy.

Cluster analysis can also be used on internal data. An approach to segmentation developed at Cranfield, for example, involves defining micro-segments based on numerous variables – who buys, what they buy, and why they buy (McDonald and Dunbar, 1995). Clusters of micro-segments that share the same, or similar, needs are then grouped together to form viable segments. Cranfield's Market Segment Master is an example of software to support this task.

Geographical information systems

Where geography is a major factor in segmentation, geographical information systems (GIS) may help by providing a graphical interface to the data using maps. Store location is a classic application of GIS, where a map interface may help to define an appropriate catchment area. Woolworth's uses CACI's InSite system to understand the local market, providing information on local population characteristics within each store's catchment area as well as information on local competitors, highlighting the potential for particular products or promotions. This information was used to segment the stores into 'city centre', 'heartland' and 'local' (Reed, 1996).

Aggregation

Once segments are defined, the data must be aggregated by segment for purposes of management information and analysis. The most problematic aspect of aggregation is dealing with cost data to provide measures of profitability by product group or market segment, involving difficult decisions on the most appropriate form of cost allocation.

4.7 MANAGEMENT INFORMATION AND CONTROL

In considering the uses to which these aggregated data are put, we examine first the provision of management information, which is the primary function of many EIS or Executive Information Systems (O'Brien, 1991). These systems provide facilities for selecting the information required and displaying it in a variety of formats, such as tables and business graphics.

Closely related to management information is management control. Performance against plan for product, market, channel and so on can be tracked through simple graphical display, or through facilities such as exception reporting, where the system highlights areas where the divergence from plan is significant.

An example of a typical system is provided by Figure 4.3. Based on an EIS product called IRI DataServer, the system allows sales information to be summarised according to a number of 'dimensions' such as product category, customer, region and time. This system, and the issues surrounding its use, are described in case E in section 7.6.

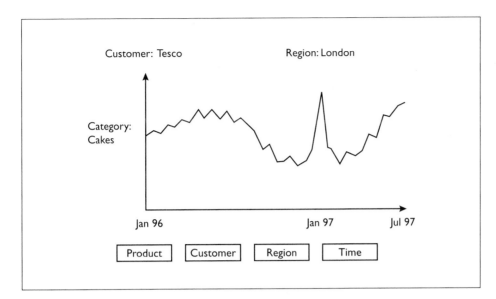

FIGURE 4.3

Management information: EIS at a food products company

Data warehousing

The IT industry has a vested interest in refreshing its vocabulary regularly to ensure that its offerings sound up to date and exciting, and are not tarred with the same brush as the previous generation, which may not have delivered all that was expected. The term 'data warehouse' has emerged in recent years as yet another label for a management information system or an EIS, most commonly (though not necessarily) focused on marketing. To be fair, the term does reflect some developments from the typical EIS of the late 1980s or early 1990s, which typically summarised a limited amount of key information in a user-friendly format:

1. Data warehouses aim to integrate data from all operational systems, such as order processing and billing, into one database using a single data model. That is, there is a single consistent view of such things as customers and products, so for example a customer's name and address will only be stored once, and all the products purchased by a customer can be readily ascertained. The data are refreshed regularly from the operational systems – typically overnight – to keep them up to date. Such data integration has long been a worthy aim of new system developments – one of the authors contributed in the early 1980s to such a large integration exercise for a utility – but the data warehousing trend has given this aim new momentum.

2. Data warehouses typically hold historical information, not just the current information needed for billing and so on. This has become possible due to the rapidly decreasing cost of computer power and storage.

3. Similarly, increasing capacity allows the information to be held at a fine level of detail. Information can be stored about individual purchases, even for mass consumer markets, over substantial periods.

Taken together, these developments provide a rich store of information which, at least potentially, integrates the two levels of data we have described – customer/product level data and aggregated data at the level of markets and product groups. As with previous generations, a range of facilities for viewing and tabulating the information may be provided, such as the SQL query language, which allows data to be collected according to specified criteria, such as 'All customers with a salary of over £40 000 and an approaching renewal date who are not currently using our highest level of service'. OLAP (on-line analytical processing) tools – again often previously called EIS or DSS – decision support systems – allow the data to be browsed graphically and tabulated in the manner of our example above.

The facilities for analysing the data bring us to the next buzzword of the moment.

Data mining

When mining, one may discover unexpected treasures – hence the term 'data mining' for searching for relevant patterns in data that had not been anticipated, such as the famous beer-and-nappies anecdote told earlier. The term tends, though, to be applied to most forms of data analysis using data warehouses. Some of the analyses of particular relevance to marketing are:

1. *segmentation*: for example, clustering routines discussed above;

2. *causal, econometric or predictive modelling*: predicting the effect on, say, future sales based on predictions of various 'input variables' such as future price, advertising spend, competitor's price and so on, discussed in section 3.5;

3. *undirected searching for correlations*: asking the system to search for significant correlations between a large number of potentially connected variables, such as consumers' purchases of particular product lines. The beer-and-nappies correlation we related earlier is an example of this: once it is discovered that certain customers tend to purchase beer and nappies and little else, the marketing executive can reflect on whether this is a nugget of information that can be put to good use, or an irrelevance.

One problem with such undirected searching is that it makes prior cost justification of the system difficult. Given that most data warehouses are in practice used more for directed searching than undirected, it seems sensible to identify in advance at least some major analyses which are likely to be of value:

> When we first put in a data warehouse in 1991, we delivered integrated data, and we had to then look for application areas that would deliver benefits. It was a huge risk for the early adopters. Today there's absolutely no excuse for taking that risk. We know exactly what the benefits are by vertical industry. In retail we can do basket analysis, we can do follow-on analysis to see if you buy x whether you buy y later on, customer value analysis to see who our best customers are, customer retention analysis to understand what are the attributes of customers who stay, margin analysis to understand the net margin, and ten other applications. Each can be looked at and cost justified on its merits. For a telephone company, on average about 65 per cent of numbers that are dialled become a billable event. The others don't get answered or whatever, and the company doesn't get their ten pence. Now if you can look at what switchboards aren't being answered, you can approach, say, a business school and say, 'last month you lost 1400 calls because the switchboards were engaged, or because people rang off after four calls. If you can improve this ratio by just one per cent you can recover the cost of the data warehouse'. So you can directly look at the applications and see whether they will indeed achieve the required benefits.
>
> Sean Kelly

We will discuss some of these analyses further in Chapter 6.

4.8 MARKETING ANALYSIS AND PLANNING

As well as providing management information and tracking performance, aggregated marketing data can be used more proactively in the formation of marketing strategy and its documentation in marketing plans. On the whole, software supporting these tasks is more sparse than for the other functions we have discussed, both in terms of the availability of commercial products and in the proportion of organisations using systems (Buttery and Tamaschke, 1995).

The functions with which systems can assist can be broadly divided into analysis, strategy formation and plan documentation. Some systems address just one of these areas, for example forecasting software. Others address more than one area: some of the few marketing planning systems in use, for example, have elements of all three.

Analysis

Software may be used to aid with the analysis of marketing information as a precursor to the formation of marketing strategy. Particular functions include the following.

Modelling

One way to understand a marketing variable of importance, such as market size or product sales, is to develop a model of the factors affecting the variable. This typically involves defining a mathematical relationship between a number of independent variables and the dependent variable whose variation is to be modelled. For example, a product sales model might include as independent variables consumer spending, product price, competitor's price, and advertising and promotion data. We showed an example of a market size model in Figure 3.7.

The model can be causal or judgemental – that is, based on the judgement of its users. As we saw in section 3.5, a causal model is built by statistical analysis of past data, most commonly through linear regression, although more recently models have also been based on neural nets (Hoptroff, 1992; Proctor, 1992). Several software routes are available for the construction of causal models. As well as general-purpose statistical packages such as SPSS (Norusis, 1993), some specialist packages are available that specifically target the business modelling market, such as the 4Thought package used in cases F and G (described in McDonald, Wilson and Hewson, 1996).

Judgemental models are based on managerial judgement rather than past data, supplemented by any hard data available. An expert consensus can be sought, for example, for predicting future uses of new technology. Another common use is to model a company's strength in a particular market through judgemental assessment of the company's performance on the market's critical success factors as one input to a portfolio analysis. In this case, the judgement is made by executives who are close to the customers in the relevant market. An example is provided in case D (and illustrated in Figure 4.4 below).

Causal models have the advantage that the model is validated against past data. Judgemental models can be less expensive to produce, and can be used where data are not available. These and other trade-offs are discussed further in Chapter 6.

A third method of building a model of market behaviour is through customer surveys or other forms of market research. This has the advantage that variables can be measured for which past data are not available, such as consumer brand perceptions. The disadvantages can include cost and sampling errors. Software for market research analysis includes questionnaire design, computer aided telephone interviewing and results analysis (Shaw, 1991).

The variable being studied does not necessarily vary with time. Cross-sectional analyses may be performed, for example comparing the effectiveness of distributors or stores, or the attractiveness of possible plant, warehouse or outlet locations (Goodchild, 1991). Those based on a time series, however, form a natural basis for forecasting, which we will now turn to.

Forecasting

Causal models can be used as a basis for forecasting. Again, regression analysis forms the dominant method: through predicting the value of the independent variables such as price, a forecast of sales or market size can be obtained. Other methods include the use of leading indicators, surveys of buyer intentions, the input/output model, and econometric models which involve the solution of multiple linear equations (Tull and Hawkins, 1984). Neural networks are again a recent addition to the armoury of techniques. The software products supporting causal modelling can typically be used for forecasting once the model is developed.

Judgemental methods can also be used, ranging from the simple aggregation of forecasts from sales representatives to the Delphi technique (Jolson and Rossow, 1971). Again, these can be cheap, and may form the only option where hard data are not available. Many bespoke operational systems allow the entry of judgemental forecasts as a basis for annual budgeting.

A third group of methods is time series analysis and projection. In this group, the forecast is based on the past values of the variable. The X-11 method, for example, analyses the time series into the underlying trend, seasonal and cyclical effects, and random perturbations. The Box–Jenkins method includes an element of judgement in that the forecaster hypothesises a relationship which is checked by the system. These methods assume that the future will be an extrapolation of the past, so are not suitable when significant changes to prices, competitive products, the legal environment and so on are expected. As with causal forecasting, a variety of software products has long been available (Wiley, 1989).

Product/market positioning

As well as examining the hard data of sales and market share, systems can assist with assessment of soft data such as a product's positioning in the marketplace. Techniques such as perceptual mapping and Porter's cost/differentiation matrix can be supported by computer to illuminate a strategy debate. A marketing planning system developed by ICL for its own use, for example, included efficiency frontier diagrams to assist with pricing, in which the relative price was plotted against a measure of the product's differentiation (Aitken and Bintley, 1989).

Portfolio positioning and balance

Portfolio models such as the BCG matrix and the directional policy matrix have been advocated for over twenty years as a means of assisting with product-market strategy and resource allocation decisions between product markets. Based on the rationale that their use without specific computer support can be both time-consuming and error-prone, some systems have appeared that help with the mechanics of portfolio analysis, and in some cases generate advice based on textbook marketing theory (reviewed by Waalewijn and Boulan, 1990, and McDonald, Wilson and Hewson, 1996).

Strategy formation

Systems providing analysis support may also allow the online modelling of the impact of proposed strategies to provide more active support for strategy formation. Perhaps the simplest form is 'gap analysis' of the gap between the forecast performance and the desired performance. Systems may also provide facilities for exploring possible strategies through 'what-if' amendments to a model. Conclusions reached about marketing objectives, strategies and tactics may be recorded. In theory, the reaction of competitors to the organisation's actions can be modelled using ideas such as gaming theory or role-playing, but in practice, such active simulation is mainly currently used for training purposes on sample data, using gaming software such as MARKSTRAT (Perry and Euler, 1989).

Systematic schemes for the evaluation of new product proposals have been developed by authors such as Cooper (1981). These lend themselves to automation as a means of guiding managers through the evaluation process. Systems have been developed by Cooper (termed NewProd and, later, DanProd) and others (Arnold and Penn, 1987), for example Cranfield's more recent New Product Manager. Systems such as Ideafisher can also be used for new product idea generation (Hirst, 1991a).

An example of a bespoke system developed to aid in strategy formation is the R&D planning system illustrated by Figure 4.4. Developed by an international pharmaceuticals company, it is designed to support the decision making of a cross-functional group of managers about the vital issue of which R&D projects to back, in an industry where development costs are enormous and time to market can easily be a decade. A core analysis is the directional policy matrix, based on judgemental inputs gathered internationally in order to ensure buy-in to the results. This summarises the potential of each project as well as the company's strength in the product area. Other analyses cover issues such as development risk and financial flows. Benefits reported by its users are greater consensus due to a depoliticised debate around a common framework, and a better corporate memory of the basis on which decisions have been taken. The facilitator reported that vital success factors were the involvement of users in the system's development as well as in data input, and the definition of the right cross-functional team to debate the model and take the appropriate decisions.

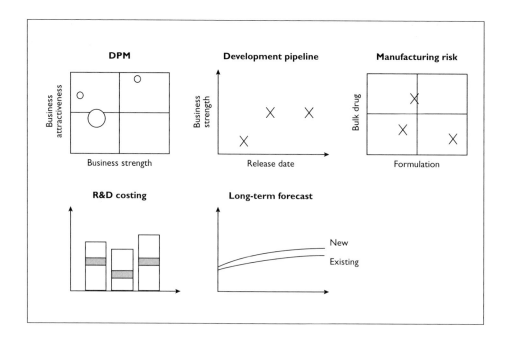

Plan documentation

Once marketing strategies have been decided, these may be documented in a marketing plan, or in a plan for one component of the marketing mix. A few systems aim to assist with this process through automatic generation of a 'template' plan which the user can then edit as necessary. Cranfield's EXMAR system adopts this approach, also including a range of tools for analysis and strategy formation, such as SWOT analysis, perceptual maps, the directional policy matrix and Boston matrix, Porter's cost/differentiation matrix and gap analysis. Systems may also aid with plan distribution through electronic mail or through adding the numerical data to management information systems.

4.9 SUMMARY

We have broken down the applications of IT in marketing into numerous parts and briefly described what is available in each. Although this was a necessary exercise, the very diversity of the field we have thereby surveyed shows why we felt it necessary to develop the simple Six 'I's framework which we are finding is valuable for communicating across the divide between marketing and IT about the strategic purposes with which IT is being asked to assist.

Electronic commerce is one particular area where effective dialogue across functions is difficult. Examples of leaders in the field can be readily understood, but deciding on the relevance of these to a given organisation is less easy. In the next chapter, we take a simple view of the field for marketing and general managers, endeavouring to answer the question: under what circumstances should I be using the Internet as a marketing and sales channel?

5

When to use
the Internet

5.1 INTRODUCTION

In a way, the Internet is simply another medium for communicating with customers, along with alternatives such as mail, the telephone and face-to-face meetings. This point is apparent, for example, in the map in Chapter 4 (*see* Figure 4.1). We have so far concentrated on issues which cut across all these media, such as how integrated data on customers can provide a basis for an interactive dialogue leading to individualised products and services, although many of our examples have included the Internet channel. So what else is there to convey in a separate chapter? Our interviews suggest that general marketing practitioners are in need of particular guidance on the Internet, not at a detailed level – to which they can often turn to resident experts or specialist reports – but in terms of when it is appropriate to consider its use. It is this specific question that we endeavour to address simply here. Our analysis is, inevitably, tentative as this relatively new medium evolves.

The current popularity of the term 'e-business' as an alternative to 'e-commerce' emphasises that wide area networks in general, and the Internet in particular, can be used for any number of applications which involve communicating with people or organisations. Our focus here is naturally on marketing – in particular, the use of the Internet as a communications medium with prospects, a sales channel and a means of product/service delivery.

Over the technical backbone of the Internet a variety of types of communication are possible, including e-mail, discussion groups, electronic data interchange from computer to computer, online advertisements and Web sites. For simplicity our emphasis here is on the role of company Web sites in communicating with their customers. But it is worth noting that even without a Web site, virtually every organisation's products are being discussed anyway in discussion groups and one-to-one e-mail conversations – by customers exchanging views, by influencers such as journalists and consultants, and by prospective customers searching for information. The issue, then, is clearly not to decide whether to be involved, but to determine the most appropriate extent of the organisation's involvement with the Internet and its place in the mix of channels.

5.2 WHEN IS THE INTERNET APPLICABLE?

The appropriateness of the Internet for a particular customer interaction will inevitably vary according to circumstances, and in particular according to the characteristics of the segment. Classic segmentation theory (McDonald and Dunbar, 1995) suggests that the channel may form a primary basis of segmentation, or in other cases a single segment may be served by several channels. Naturally, individual customers will also have their own channel preferences, and often it may be necessary to leave the choice to the customer. In general, though, cases where the Internet will be appropriate can be anticipated by considering whether its features match the needs of the interaction. We discuss some of the main features here.

When the connected subset fits the target market

As long as the Internet is accessible by only a proportion of the population, it is clearly relevant to determine what proportion of the target segment have access. Although users have long since moved beyond the nerd stereotype, there is still a bias towards more highly educated, affluent consumers and, in the business-to-business sector, professionals using computers regularly such as those in the IT industry. Age is less a factor than commonly assumed: a 1997 US survey by McKinsey, for example, found that 43 per cent of highly paid men aged 35 to 44 had used the Internet in the preceding month, a figure approaching a critical mass, whereas only 20 per cent of 18–24 year olds had – reflecting, perhaps, lower use at work in this age group. Gender has also become less important. In the McKinsey study, 21 per cent of women earners aged 25 to 34 were users against 26 per cent of men of the same age. By 1998, more than half of new US Net customers were female (Gens, 1999). IDC predicts that the 150 million Net users in March 1999, up from 20 million in 1995, will grow to half a billion by 2003, boosted by interactive television and mobile phone Net links.

The UK lags behind the US in Internet usage. An ICM poll in January 1999 (Travis, 1999) showed that 29 per cent of British adults were online, with a further 14 per cent planning to get access within the next year. Twenty per cent had access at work, with a peak among the 25–34 age group at 33 per cent, and a trough among manual workers at 4 per cent. Fourteen per cent were connected at home against 27 per cent in the US. Again, a class distinction was evident, with a third of ABs online at home against 16 per cent of C1s and 2 per cent of DEs. This suggests that the UK has now entered the 'early majority' stage on Everrett Rogers' classic diffusion of innovation model, which we have applied to the Internet in Figure 5.1.

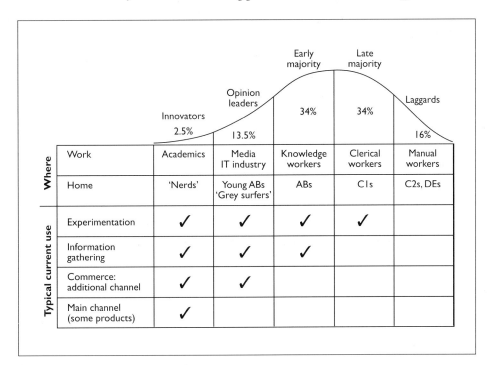

FIGURE 5.1

The Internet: diffusion of innovation

As Figure 5.1 also illustrates, as the number of connected users grows, so does the extent of use by each user, as experimental browsing proceeds via serious information gathering to online purchasing. IDC's figures are for $900 bn of e-commerce by 2003. (For up-to-date statistics on Net use see *www.nua.org/surveys*.) The quality of the connection is a relevant factor in the speed with which a user passes through these stages: many business users have high-speed links which reduce an important barrier to the Internet's utility – the slow response times that can annoy the user into switching to other media.

Another factor is learning on the part of suppliers: until Web sites are faster, more reliable and have more complete functionality, e-commerce is held back from achieving its full potential. A UK Web site survey found that almost half of the attempts to access some of the UK's most popular electronic banking sites failed, while others took over a minute to download a page. The variation was high: while 99 per cent of visits to Midland's site were successful, only 57 per cent of connection attempts to Citibank's were (Ranger, 1999).

Some useful research by leading UK academics (Lockett and Littler, 1997) has elicited some of the characteristics of early adopters of a related innovation: direct banking by telephone. It found that early adopters have a higher degree of opinion leadership and have a more favourable attitude towards change than non-adopters. The most important perceived atttribute of direct banking is 24-hour availability, outweighing for the adopters negative attributes such as perceived complexity and risk of the service.

This research has obvious parallels for Internet-based product and service delivery. A careful study of Internet users (Jarvenpaa and Todd, 1997) found that, contrary to common belief, the availability of products at the right price, and the convenience of buying in terms of time, shopping enjoyment and customer service, were more important factors in determining whether shoppers used the Internet than the perceived risk associated with giving credit card details online. While security and privacy are issues, users are usually willing to trade them for some perceived economic or other benefit.

When you need asynchronous communication at a distance

Unlike a sales call, the communication can be carried out at any distance, a particular benefit for geographically dispersed markets and those where the cost of sales visits is prohibitive. Asynchronicity means that those communicating do not need to do so at the same time; hence Internet banking can be provided throughout the night without the additional cost of employing staff at antisocial hours, and product support by electronic mail can be provided when the local staff are next in the office. When required, though, Internet communications can be synchronous: an example is providing a button on a Web site to 'Talk to a representative', leading to a live telephone or video link – facilities which will soon be common (Black, 1999).

When you need interactivity (and the interactions are programmable)

The Internet is more interactive than direct mail or broadcast media such as traditional (non-interactive) television – at least in principle. We saw from our discussion of Dell in section 3.3 that much of the real potential of the Internet is from interactive communication so as to understand customers and personalise the offering. But the current dominant reality of

Web sites on the Net is the 'brochureware' that does little more than provide an online version of a product brochure, as a recent study of Times 500 companies reported:

> We found that the vast majority of those organisations surveyed were not engaging in any form of interactive marketing. Their web sites were merely operating at the most basic level, providing passive information. Almost half of the web sites we visited did not request any personal details from visitors. Of those that did, only a tenth asked for anything more meaningful than name and phone number. It seems that most UK organisations have failed to grasp the basic elements of salesmanship, that is talking to, and more importantly listening to, customers.
>
> (Cambridge Technology Group, 1998)

Interactivity on a Web site differs in nature from that of the telephone or the sales visit, in that the interaction is with a computer rather than a person. This is appropriate for high-volume, repetitive interactions where a computer can be programmed to perform the task. To take the Dell case again, configuring a computer is one of the few tasks where expert systems have matched their early promise, being the kind of well-specified task that computers are good at, but with sufficient detail and complexity to be cumbersome and error-prone for humans. Computers are also good at arithmetic, and the customer can see the price of a package interactively as items are added to the bundle. But other interactive tasks still require a human: configuring of a complex software package such as an accounting application, for example – hence the dominance of the face-to-face sales model in sales of software development and consultancy services.

We have seen that a precursor to interaction is integration of customer data – a fact often lost on companies which delegate the Web site to enthusiasts in an isolated corner of the organisation, or outsource its development and operations with minimal provision for information transfer – hence repeating the mistakes often made in the early days of the call centre (Vernon, 1999).

When sight and sound are adequate

The Web is mainly a medium of two-dimensional static words and graphics, though this is expanding as bandwidth issues are addressed to include sound and video, and doubtless will expand further in the future. This makes certain products less appropriate for sale over the Net, such as clothes where the customer may wish to feel the fabric or try the item on – though routine or repeat purchases of clothes such as jeans or underwear are being targeted for Internet sales.

When you can benefit from low variable costs

The electrical components company RS Components, traditionally a catalogue seller, is achieving growth through its Web channel without the need to expand its call centre proportionately (Price, 1999). The corporate foreign exchange section of Thomas Cook is finding and serving new customers through its Web site which it could not possibly serve with its traditional salesforce. The variable cost of the Internet as a communication mechanism can be relatively low.

For most media, the more specific the targeting of a campaign, the higher the cost per thousand. Billboards are seen by a lot of people, only some of whom are relevant to the campaign. A mailshot is expensive but can be very specifically targeted. But once a Web site exists, and assuming that the users can be motivated to look at it, the variable cost of the interaction can be very low.

One major fixed cost is the development of the Web site and related back-end software. Fortune 500 companies spent $800 000 to $1.5 million just to get their Web sites up and running, according to a Gartner survey (Phillips et al., 1997). This balance suits cases where volumes are high. UPS, for example, claims considerable savings from the 60 000 customers per day who check the status of their parcel delivery online, saving 30 cents each time in telephone operator time. The conventional wisdom that one is saved the necessity of advertising – that the customer comes to you – is, however, often false, though it has a grain of truth. The online search engines and directories give prominence to particular sites which have spent heavily to gain their place in the hierarchy or the prominence of their banner advertisement. If you wish to sell your greetings cards online, you may have to pay an online bookstore well to have a link to your Web site from its order form.

To deliver 'infoware' products and services

'Infoware' can be delivered electronically down a telephone line. If the product itself is information, it can be delivered using the Internet. Examples are weather reports, share prices, books and reports, news, software, music and videos. But even physical products often have an 'information surround' where value can be added to the core product. The IT industry, for example, uses the Internet extensively for providing product support. Common faults on a Hewlett Packard printer can be diagnosed by the user without taking up expensive telephone support operators' time. The large computer companies such as HP also produce online briefings on developments in the computer field for the benefit of their professional IT customers, as a small added-value service that keeps customers coming back to the Web site and enhances the company image.

Newspapers provide an interesting example of infoware. Newspapers compete with a variety of media: TV and radio for news, magazines for advertisements, telephones and faxes for weather forecasts. As Evans and Wurster (1997) hypothesise, the vertical integration of the newspaper, integrating journalists, editors, printing and distribution in one organisation, may break down under the new threat of electronic news distribution – perhaps along the lines of Figure 5.2. New online intermediaries are providing an alternative link between news originators and the customer, collecting information from the customer on what news they are interested in and packaging a response. The CNN Web site has an addition called Custom News which allows users to personalise the news they receive. Yahoo's Full Coverage service takes a mix of Reuters feeds and links to other sites to provide a viable first port of call for news (*www.yahoo.com/Full-Coverage*). Advertisers can pay for their products to be advertised along with relevant news stories – Manchester United kit along with a match report – or the customer may request product information – a 'pull' request. Although the newspaper as a remarkably cheap means of distributing vast quantities of information remains secure for the present, the market is already changing: fewer young people read newspapers, as they turn to other sources for news and information – the Internet for advertisements for houses (*www.uk-property.com*), jobs (*www.jobworld.co.uk*) and cars (*www.exchangeandmart.co.uk*) and for weather reports (*weather.yahoo.com*), for example. For the time being the newspapers are not finding the Internet a lucrative channel for their traditional integrated product: *The Times* offers a full annual service for a £100 fee, but regards its purpose as mainly promotional and experimental, though respectable advertising revenues have been growing for some time (Kavanagh, 1997).

FIGURE 5.2

The future of news provision

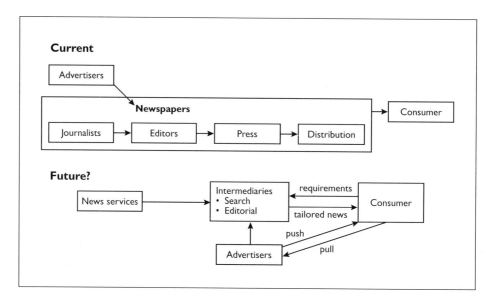

When privacy and security concerns are not dominant

The use of the Internet for the actual placement of an order is being held back by user concerns about security. While these are being addressed through initiatives such as the SET protocol for credit card payments, this has to date biased Internet sales in the direction of relatively low-value items and in favour of suppliers with strong brands trusted by the consumer. Users may also have concerns about the privacy of the information they provide. But as we have seen, market research into Internet use suggests that, while security and privacy remain genuine concerns, the dominant factors affecting whether the Internet is used remain the traditional factors of shopping experience: price, convenience, service levels, product availability and so on. Hence the more mundane issues of improving the Internet's speed and the quality of Web sites will be as important as addressing the higher-profile security issues in determining its growth over the next few years.

5.3 EXAMPLE: AMAZON.COM BOOKS

To illustrate these principles, the best-known exponent of Internet marketing, the bookseller Amazon.com, is worth examining as it shows simply the terrain on which many other industries are now having to fight. Amazon exploits the Web's interactive nature by offering facilities such as: searching for books on particular topics; tracking the status of an order placed earlier; making recommendations of books based on a list of the user's favourites; and providing reviews of a book placed by other customers. The Web site builds knowledge of the customer, enabling it for example to notify the customer by e-mail if a new book appears on a topic of particular interest.

Amazon's rapid growth took it from revenue of $16 m in 1996 (*Economist*, 1997), representing 3 per cent of e-commerce in that year, to over $100 m in 1997, during which it went public, gaining $50 m in funding. But 1997 was still unprofitable, with losses of $10 m in the first six months alone. This was little to do with the essential soundness of selling books over the Internet and everything to do with the fight with the traditional retailers as Amazon became a serious threat. The flagships of the traditional and new approaches are illustrated in Figure 5.3. Amazon's continuing difficulty in making a profit in 1998, as its sales rose to around $400 m, did not stop the stock market valuing the company by the end of the year at $17 billion, compared with $2.9 billion for Barnes & Noble, the largest US retailer.

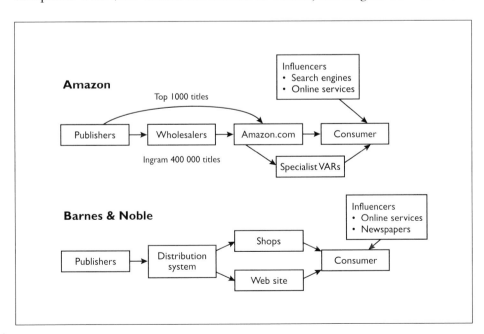

FIGURE 5.3

Independence of location: Amazon vs Barnes & Noble

Barnes & Noble launched its own Web site in March 1997. To respond, Amazon was forced to buy visibility expensively on the Net. Deals with the search engine/directories Yahoo and Excite were designed to ensure that when seeking books, users would find their way to Amazon (Moody, 1997). Barnes & Noble, meanwhile, with profits then greater than Amazon's entire turnover, made a deal with America Online (AOL), a service provider with 8.5 m subscribers, ensuring privileged access to much of their potential market. They also invested in advertising the site in papers such as the *New York Times*. Similarly, the number two US retailer Borders, with nearly $2 bn in revenue, launched its Web site later in 1997.

Barnes & Noble played me-too on its Web site, copying initiatives by Amazon as quickly as possible to neutralise its advantage. What differences remain between them? Amazon relies on the physical proximity of its offices to the largest wholesaler of books, Ingram Book Company, which stocks 400 000 titles and provides 59 per cent of Amazon sales. The 1000 top sellers are the only stock that Amazon carries itself (Lamb, 1997b). Barnes & Noble, by contrast, has its own distribution network, designed for supplying its shops, with huge stocks, often enabling it to get books out faster than Amazon. Amazon is also vulnerable to competition from other Web-based retailers who draw on the same wholesalers, such as Bookstacks and Bookserve.

Amazon continues to innovate in an attempt to maintain its differentiation. It extended its 'top 20' listing of bestselling books to include every book listed on the Web site, providing an endless source of depressing news for authors of niche items who might discover their masterpiece at number 4503 in the bestseller list. In an attempt to compete with niche sellers such as Pandora's books, which sells out-of-print sci-fi (again with Ingram's assistance), Amazon set up an associates programme, whereby any other site – say, a business school's – can point its Web site visitors to Amazon.com to buy books by its faculty in exchange for 8 per cent of the resulting revenue. It is now diversifying into sales of CDs and videos, and recently launched an auction service where users can auction virtually anything.

The details of this fight are rapidly changing, but whatever the result, the story illustrates some of the points we have made about Internet selling. Books are low in price, reducing security concerns. Most purchasers do not feel the need to see the book itself or read extracts: often they know what they want, or are prepared to take a risk based on the title, the publisher's copy, reviews and recommendations. Searching a shop can be time-consuming and less efficient than searching online with the aid of a computer. The successful Web sellers are adding value through facilities such as logging your own review and reading those of others. And the myth that all participants in the online market have equal share of voice is shown to be false, the fight for visibility being an expensive one.

The comparison with the US illustrates how the UK lags the US in Internet usage. The relatively well-established site of Blackwell's (*bookshop.blackwells.co.uk*) had made just £500 000 in sales by September 1997 (Kim, 1997). The UK-based Internet Bookshop was purchased by WH Smith for around £15 m, before it had clocked up significant sales – the purchase being based on the investment by WH Smith that was thereby saved. WH Smith further boosted their Internet credentials in an Internet-obsessed stock market by purchasing Helicon Publishing, which produces reference material including an online encyclopedia, which it intends to use in a relaunched site in 1999 (Cope, 1999). Amazon themselves took over another relatively small online UK bookstore, Bookpages, relaunching in 1998 as *Amazon.co.uk*. Some of these sites have lagged behind the US leaders in reliability and sophistication, reflecting their as yet smaller markets.

5.4 SUMMARY

We have examined some of the criteria that determine whether a given customer interaction is suitable for use on the Web. We illustrate a formal analysis using such criteria which we have found useful in Figure 5.4. In this example for a hypothetical segment of the book market, the customers wish to: browse for the book they want; ideally view at least the cover and copy for the book; complete their purchase with as much convenience as possible (saving a journey to a shop if they can); and buy at low cost. The 'accessibility' factor represents the fact that they cannot use a medium that is not available to them, as will be the case for some members of the segment as far as the Internet is concerned. Having determined the customers' buying criteria, ideally by market research, the various possible media can then be assessed against these criteria. For this segment, the bar charts suggest that shops and the Net are more likely shopping destinations than catalogues or the telephone. It is important to note that needs will vary between segments: another segment of, say, senior management purchasing management reports in the workplace may tend to know what book they want, have very demanding requirements for convenience, ruling out a special shop visit, and be less price sensitive.

FIGURE 5.4

Choosing channels: channel matrix

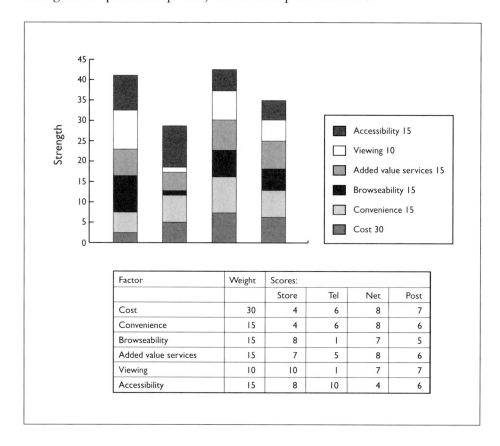

Factor	Weight	Scores:			
		Store	Tel	Net	Post
Cost	30	4	6	8	7
Convenience	15	4	6	8	6
Browseability	15	8	1	7	5
Added value services	15	7	5	8	6
Viewing	10	10	1	7	7
Accessibility	15	8	10	4	6

Such an analysis is probably largely unnecessary in the book market, for which the strengths and weaknesses of the Internet as a channel are well established. But whether this analysis is carried out formally, based on market research, or more intuitively, some such thought process is vital for those markets where the Web is as yet relatively unimportant in order to determine how extensively, and how soon, to invest – although for increasing numbers of industries, the potential of the Web is being revealed all too clearly by industry leaders who have added the Web as a further channel, or by new Internet-based competitors who are stealing market share from established players.

6

Software for analysis and planning

6.1 INTRODUCTION

We have looked at one specific aspect of IT in marketing, the Internet, and its use for electronic commerce. In this chapter we look in some detail at another area: the use of software to support marketing analysis and planning decisions. This chapter complements the review in section 4.8 of the software available by comparing and contrasting some of the major styles of support to guide practitioners as to when each is appropriate.

6.2 MARKETING PLANNING SOFTWARE: A SIMPLIFIED TYPOLOGY

This section defines a simplified and non-exhaustive typology of categories of marketing planning system that are commonly found in practice.

Table 6.1 lists the five types, with some examples of each. Systems within each type are divided into software products (the first three columns) and bespoke systems (the last column). The software products are further categorised according to whether the system is targeted primarily at marketing, at business/corporate planning or at any problem-solving application ('generic'). The case letters refer to our case studies described in Chapter 7. Before comparing the approaches we will describe them in more detail.

Type	*Targeting* Marketing	Corporate	Generic	Bespoke
Planning systems for multiple product markets	EXMAR			Case D (Figure 4.4)
Planning systems for one product/business unit		Business Insight (case H) ANSPLAN		Assist (ICI)
Causal modelling			4Thought (cases F, G) SPSS	
Data consolidation and display	DataServer (case E)			
Individual marketing techniques	Portfolio Planner New Product Manager		HiView Equity COPE	Marketing Workbench (ICL)

TABLE 6.1

A typology of systems contributing to marketing planning

Planning systems for multiple product markets

These systems aim to assist with the definition and documentation of marketing strategy for a business unit with several product markets. In addition to any analyses per product market, they therefore may include comparison of the attractiveness or potential of the product markets and aggregation of individual product-market figures to produce data at the level of the business unit. In common with the next type, their typical approach to market modelling (as discussed in section 4.8) can be characterised as judgemental rather than causal, although some inputs may in practice be derived from causal modelling or market research.

Cranfield's EXMAR system is an example of this system type, targeted at marketing. It guides the user through a marketing planning process, prompting for key data, using marketing techniques such as perceptual maps and portfolio matrices to aid understanding, and supporting the documentation of resulting strategies in a marketing plan. An example of a bespoke system is shown in Figure 4.4. Another bespoke system seen by the authors which was developed for an animal health company includes SWOT analysis and portfolio analysis. Marketing Director from Director Portfolio (Newing, 1995) is another product in this category.

Planning systems for one product/business unit

These systems assist with planning for one product, product market or business unit. While the systems can be used twice on different product markets, they do not aim to assist with issues of resource allocation or synergy between product markets. Typically aimed either at product managers or general managers, examples are Business Insight, an expert system incorporating a number of marketing and strategy theories (McNeilly and Gessner, 1993); the ANSPLAN system, which includes a portfolio matrix analysis but for one product market or business unit at a time; and ICI's Assist, an internally developed system demonstrated to the authors which asks the user a series of questions about a product market and then generates advice, drawing on specific knowledge of the chemical industry coded into the program. While the usage of Assist was initially significant in terms of numbers of business units, it tended to be used once only to generate ideas in a single session. It is believed to have fallen into disuse, due to a combination of factors including its applicability only to certain bulk chemical industries and the technology used.

As with the multiple product-market systems, these systems may include several of the functions included under Analysis, Strategy formation and Plan documentation in Figure 4.1, but exclude issues of portfolio balance.

Causal modelling

These systems support regression or equivalent techniques for modelling such variables as market size and market share. We described these systems in sections 3.5 and 4.8 (*see* particularly Figure 3.7). The 4Thought system is discussed in cases F and G. Other packages incorporating linear regression include the main statistical packages such as SPSS. These systems correspond to the modelling and forecasting functions in Figure 4.1, though specialist forecasting packages are also available.

Data consolidation and display

These systems correspond to the management information and management control functions in Figure 4.1, which as we have discussed come under labels including EIS (Executive Information Systems) and OLAP (On-Line Analytical Processing). One of the many examples is IRI's DataServer, studied in case E (and illustrated in Figure 4.3), which is targeted specifically at marketing. A large number of others is reviewed in McDonald, Wilson and Hewson (1996).

Individual marketing techniques

These systems support individual marketing tools and techniques, with little or no attempt to integrate the tools or to provide a planning framework. The key benefit offered is typically the graphical presentation of the data to aid understanding, in some cases supplemented by advice based on the underlying theory for the technique. Examples are portfolio matrix drawing tools such as Portfolio Planner from Marketing Improvements, MatMar from Automated Marketing Systems and Portfolio-Plus from Strategic Dynamics, and new product evaluation tools, discussed above. Software can be obtained for generic decision support techniques such as the Analytic Hierarchy Process, for example HiView (Peterson, 1994), Equity (Phillips, 1989) and COPE, which supports Eden's (1989) cognitive-mapping-based SODA methodology. The ICL system discussed earlier incorporated several marketing tools, but without integration round a planning process – in the words of its principal sponsor, without a 'washing line to hang the pegs on'.

Conclusions

We have presented a simple typology of systems contributing to marketing planning. The most mature of the marketing planning system types we have defined is data consolidation and display systems, with causal modelling systems also being moderately common, particularly in FMCG organisations. Of the remainder, support for individual marketing techniques is more common than their integrated support within a wider planning process. We will now turn to comparing these approaches.

6.3 COMPARISON OF APPROACHES

We first compare the system benefits and success factors from case studies carried out for this report and in previous research at Cranfield. Table 6.2 summarises the main benefits for three of the system types. We have combined the 'planning systems for one product/business unit' and 'planning systems for multiple product/markets' under the heading of 'judgement-based planning systems', as their analyses of the workings of a market typically emphasise managerial judgement (as, for example, in definition of critical success factors, weights and scores) rather than hard numeric data.

TABLE 6.2

Benefits of different approaches to planning

Data consolidation/display systems (EIS etc.)	Causal modelling systems	Judgement-based planning systems
Update intuition through graphical display and interactive specification of data	Update intuition through modelling of factors driving marketing variables	Aid use of marketing tools through calculations, graphical display, guidance on use
Information availability and accuracy	Enable aspects of live marketing model	Aid identification of data requirements
Improve decision justification, credibility and confidence	Improve decision justification, credibility and confidence	Improve plan justification, credibility and confidence
Time savings on information retrieval		Support group planning, focusing debate and improving consensus

Benefits of data consolidation and display systems such as case E are, naturally enough, focused on the availability, accuracy and timeliness of data. While the concept of 'updating of the users' intuition' applies to these systems as well as to judgement-based planning systems, here the users' understanding of the workings of the market is challenged simply through the graphical display of data on market size and sales figures aggregated in diverse ways, and through the ability to explore the reasons for patterns in data by 'drilling down' to a finer level of detail.

In contrast, in causal modelling, this role of challenging the managers' current understanding is carried out through a statistical model. Like the judgement-based planning systems, they allow a move towards continuously updated marketing models, with snapshots being taken for annual planning purposes. Being based on regularly collected time series data, such a model can be updated by exception when market conditions change, as case F shows, rather than in response to an annual planning cycle.

The benefits shown by planning systems for one product/business unit (such as case H) do not differ significantly from the benefits of multiple product-market systems, with the exception that the marketing tools supported by the former tend to emphasise business unit strategy, such as Porter's generic strategies, rather than issues of portfolio balance and synergies between product markets. The particular system studied in case H also has quite an expert systems flavour, being more proactive in offering advice than, say, Cranfield's EXMAR. While this was found to be useful in providing a further means by which the user's understanding could be challenged, a trade-off was that it was not always easy to understand the reasoning for the advice given. Trust in the system was therefore more of an issue than with the systems which put more of the onus of interpretation onto the user.

Turning to success factors which determine whether the system's application is successful (*see* Table 6.3), data consolidation and display systems are often used by individual product managers, rather than by a team. Here, the equivalent of the 'sufficiently wide team definition' found in judgement-based planning systems is 'sufficiently wide system availability', as the multiple ways in which the data can be analysed are of relevance to different groups for different decisions. As with other system types, the appropriate definition of product and market hierarchies is an essential precursor to analysis.

Data consolidation/display systems (EIS etc.)	Causal modelling systems	Judgement-based planning systems
Adequate training	Supportive culture	System champion and sponsor
Sufficiently wide system availability	Availability of modelling expertise	Ease of use
Co-ordination of system use with planning cycle	Appropriate definition of market segments	Sufficiently wide team definition
Appropriate analysis units	Co-ordination with planning cycle	System perceived as empowering not controlling
		Appropriate planning units

Causal modelling systems similarly depend on appropriate definition of market segments, some results in case G being questioned on the basis of whether segments were in fact distinct. One difference from the judgement-based planning systems is that the model can be defined by an expert without the involvement of relevant managers, though of course the results must then be presented to those involved in the market. The equivalent of the 'adequate facilitation' found essential for judgement-based planning systems is therefore the availability of a user with sufficient statistical knowledge to define inputs and interpret the results, as well as the ability to run the system.

6.4 APPROACHES TO MARKET MODELLING: A COMPARISON

We have seen that the various system types exhibit different benefits and different success factors for achieving them. This is, of course, a reflection of their differing functions. For example, the data consolidation and display systems have a strong role in control of progress against the annual plan, whereas other planning software concentrates on plan creation. But in one respect, several of the system types can perform what at a broad level is the same function: the modelling of the workings of a market and the various competitors' strengths and weaknesses, as a basis for decision making about marketing strategy and tactics. When, then, should one system type be used rather than another? Some guidelines are shown in Table 6.4.

Approach	Judgement-based	Causal modelling	Descriptive (data display)
Applicability to:			
Analysis	Group hypothesis consolidation	Hypothesis testing	Hypothesis generating (individual)
Forecasting	Uncertain data	When data available	Extrapolation – when past = future (values as well as variables)
	NPD, changing markets	When past = future (variables driving market, not necessarily values)	
Strategy/tactics formation	Portfolio strategy; overall product-market strategy	Marketing mix fine-tuning	Current/historic size/sales as baseline for planning
Control	Regular/annual: review of strategy	Continuous: market departing from model	Continuous: sales departing from plan
Other selection criteria:			
Data requirements	Low: views of managers close to market	High: hard data, all relevant variables	Medium: hard data, sales/market size
Threats to validity	'Conventional wisdom' biases in culture	Causality vs association: choice of variables	Disentangling causality: subjective interpretation
Threats to acceptability	Rejection as pseudo-science	Communicability; presence of statistics skills	Computer use in daily role of product managers

TABLE 6.4

Approaches to market modelling: applicability

Analysis

Data consolidation and display systems act as generators of hypotheses about the workings of the market as users, typically working on their own, explore the reasons for a peak or a trough in market sales or market size. These hypotheses (often regarded as 'facts' by the users) can be tested more rigorously through the use of a causal model, which assesses the relevance of each hypothesised variable in predicting sales or market size. A judgement-based model, by contrast, allows the views of several managers to be consolidated, for example in a list of critical success factors, weights and scores. The logic of such an approach is that the managers will have different experience and knowledge which, when combined, is likely to lead to a better model than that obtained from one manager alone.

Forecasting

Descriptive systems can only forecast with accuracy if the future is an extrapolation of the past. This implies both that the same variables (such as promotions, advertising spend and price) are driving the market, and that their values either remain constant or will continue to change much as they have in the past. By contrast, causal models can still produce an accurate prediction if values of relevant variables change radically – for example, in the wake of a change in pricing strategy from a competitor. If the nature of the market changes, however – as, for example, when a new factor emerges such as product safety following a well-publicised safety scare – a causal model will not be able to make predictions until a number of months of data is available. In these situations, and in other situations where data are uncertain or unavailable such as in entirely new markets, judgement-based modelling offers a more structured alternative to individual 'gut feel'.

Strategy/tactics formation

Descriptive systems can simply offer current and historic data to form a baseline for planning at whatever level of product market is required. Apart from producing more robust forecasts, causal models can allow the modelling of particular proposed alterations to the marketing mix, such as the optimal level of pricing. Because judgement-based models can include 'soft' variables for which data are rarely available, such as product quality, service and image, they can form the basis for the wider definition of product-market strategy, as well as for issues of resource allocation between a number of product markets for which causal models may not be available.

Control

Because of their subjective nature, judgement-based models cannot be continuously monitored against reality without the reconvening of the group that arrived at the model. The appropriate way to update such models is therefore through a regular review process, either as part of an annual planning cycle or at more frequent intervals (as in the bi-annual reviews of the pharmaceuticals company of Figure 4.4). As case F illustrates, causal models can, by contrast, be automatically monitored against reality, with an update to the model being triggered when new data do not fit with its predictions. The control role of descriptive systems is more commonly to monitor sales against plan, and where there is a divergence, to use 'drill-down' facilities to examine where the divergence occurs.

Data requirements

The approaches vary in their requirements for information. Judgement-based models are based on the views of those managers who have knowledge of the market in question, supplemented by harder data where available. As with the informal conclusions reached by users of descriptive models, judgement-based models can only be tested informally against hard data. Descriptive systems require, however, at least the availability of sales data, and often market size data as well. Causal models require data on all relevant variables, including variables such as advertising spend. These can be hard to come by, and may require considerable creativity in their definition.

Threats to validity

The potentials for bias differ between the three types of market modelling. Judgement-based models can be subject to biases due to a culture where certain 'conventional wisdom' tenets are held to be self-evident (case G). In these cases, the averaging effect of involving several managers deemed to possess relevant knowledge may not approach the market reality. Although based on hard data, interpretations made by users of descriptive systems – as, for example, on the reason for a dip in sales being an advertising campaign by a competitor – are subject to difficulties in disentangling the effects of various variables which may be changing simultaneously. This subjectivity of interpretation is not a problem with causal models, where statistics are available on the relative weight of different variables. However, the choice of variables is still subject to judgement, as is the interpretation of an association between two variables which may be due to a common third cause rather than a direct causal link.

Threats to acceptability

Some other factors have been noted that may influence the acceptability of systems. Judgement-based modelling may be dismissed in some particularly data-based cultures as 'pseudo-scientific' (as suggested by case F). While such cultures are likely to approve of causal modelling, this approach may in other cases be regarded as academic and incomprehensible, as explaining the outputs is not always easy (case G). A further barrier to the acceptance of causal modelling is the need for statistical expertise to define and interpret the models. The transparency of data consolidation and display systems is not subject to these problems of the believability of the system's outputs; however, as their power lies in the constant availability of updated information as a basis for control and hypothesis generation, one threat to acceptability lies in the need for wider system usage than with the other system types. Case E illustrates that not all product managers will necessarily take naturally to such systems.

Implications for software design

Some pointers towards appropriate design features to support these approaches to market modelling are provided in Table 6.5.

TABLE 6.5

Approaches to market modelling: software design issues

Approach Issue	Judgement-based planning systems	Causal modelling	Descriptive (data display)
Input data	Structured and unstructured	Structured	Structured
Models/data manipulation	SWOT analysis/CSFs, portfolio matrices, perceptual maps, etc.	Regression Solution of multiple linear equations	Consolidation/data slicing
Outputs	Graphical display, advice	Equations, graphical display	Graphical display, tables
Group support	Combining/contrasting perspectives	–	Data distribution
Integration	Office automation systems, e.g. word processing	Models at higher and lower levels of aggregation	Operational systems (sales data); external databases (market size)
Users	Marketing managers plus management team, facilitated	Specialists reporting to marketing/ product managers	Market/product/brand managers, account managers
Tools/traditions	DSS Office automation	Statistics Spreadsheets	EIS DBMS
Bespoke vs. off-shelf	Either, but off-shelf core likely to be lower risk	Off-shelf (ad hoc) Tailored/off-shelf (regular forecasting)	EIS shell tailored with hierarchies and data feeds
Development risks	Specification Ease of use	Ease of use	Software design, e.g. sizing, performance Ease of use

Data

Judgement-based systems require a variety of types of data. The directional policy matrix, for example, requires 'structured' sales data for the circle size, 'semi-structured' assessment of strength in market and market attractiveness, and 'unstructured' words to document such factors as the reasons for scores given and assumptions made. The importance of unstructured data was mentioned in several cases. Causal models require structured data as inputs, though in some cases dummy variables may be used as an approximation – as, for example, when a competitor promotion is known to have occurred but where numeric details are not available (case G). Descriptive systems use straightforward structured data, concentrating on sales and market size – though one user requested the ability to annotate the data with notes on plausible interpretations for variations and so on.

Models/data manipulation

The judgement-based models such as portfolio analysis involve simple calculations and graphical display. Causal modelling naturally has a greater emphasis on data manipulation through techniques such as linear regression, or (in the case of more sophisticated econometric models) the solution of multiple simultaneous linear equations. Descriptive systems simply consolidate the data or allow them to be broken down into their component parts.

Outputs

Judgement-based models often concentrate on graphical display to avoid the potentially spurious accuracy of numeric outputs and as a vehicle for communication. Advice based on the underlying marketing theory is an optional component whose utility was cited in case H. While causal models may also provide graphical display to illustrate the outcome, the primary result is the equation, or equations, relating the variables. Descriptive systems add value through the tabulation or graphical display of the required information.

Group support

Causal models do not need to be used by a group, though the outputs will naturally need to be disseminated. Descriptive systems only need to support a group in so far as centrally held data are made available to a number of users; for this purpose, terminals into a mainframe or smaller server remain common. The combining and contrasting of the perspectives of different members of the management team is one of the clearest benefits of judgement-based models. None of the systems studied explicitly supported this process through multi-user facilities or the recording of different perspectives simultaneously; rather, the perspectives were informally discussed when the system prompted for a single number such as a critical success factor score, often with the system display projected onto an overhead projector screen. There may be scope for useful extensions to judgement-based systems incorporating explicit group support, such as anonymous voting and Delphi.

Integration

The most clearly requested link from judgement-based systems is to office automation applications such as word processing, spreadsheets, graphics packages and electronic mail. Outputs from judgement-based models may be included in plan documents or presentations, while further analyses or graphics may be generated using spreadsheets, and electronic mail can be used to disseminate results or to request information. Causal models may stand alone (cases F and G), though the integration of resulting forecasts in a hierarchy of product markets may be useful for regular forecasting purposes (case G). Data consolidation and display systems need to be integrated with their sources of data.

Users

The differing users of the three types of model have implications for software design issues such as user interface design. Judgement-based models are likely to be used by marketing managers, often in conjunction with other members of the senior management team and with a facilitator from outside the organisation or from the marketing department. Causal models are likely to be used by specialists while descriptive systems may be used widely by marketing and sales staff.

Tools/traditions

This entry summarises the traditions in software development on which systems draw in supporting the different types of market model. Judgement-based models draw on the tradition of DSS development, as well as the recent advances in ease of use of office automation programs. Causal models may likewise have interfaces consistent with spreadsheet look and feel standards, as well as a statistical core. Data consolidation and display systems draw on the long tradition of corporate databases, the simplicity of use and navigation pioneered by executive information systems, and the multi-dimensional databases described commercially under various terms including DSS generators, EIS shells and OLAP systems.

Bespoke vs off-the-shelf development

Some tentative pointers can be offered as to whether software development should be undertaken in-house or through the purchase of an off-the-shelf system. Although judgement-based systems can be developed relatively painlessly in-house, problems can emerge with software development, as discussed below. Where an off-the-shelf system is available with a specification meeting much of the requirement, the lack of development risk should be considered as a factor. Similar remarks apply to causal modelling, where tailored or bespoke software may be subject to development risks, particularly in ease of use (case G – a system development contrasted with the main software studied). With data consolidation and display systems, the various EIS 'shells' on the market can be tailored to the organisation.

Development risks

Ease of use is an issue for all types of system and a common area for problems in development. Judgement-based models are subject to the further risk that the specification may rely on a mature application of marketing theory and its adaptation to the organisation: only one organisation studied achieved this without at least two iterations of software development. Technical design issues such as sizing and performance are particularly important for the large amounts of data handled by descriptive systems (case H), though they have also been observed with other types of system.

6.5 SUMMARY

We have compared several approaches to software support for marketing planning. Not the most fashionable area of application of IT within marketing, this area of the domain is difficult to convey on paper to those who are not familiar with the types of system described. We can only urge such readers to examine some such systems for themselves before returning to these research results. Our research has, however, shown that real benefits can be obtained through the embedding of best-practice planning procedures via software, through the insights thus gained into the workings of markets and one's place within them, and through the consequent wider commitment to a common course of action that can be derived from an analysis in which the whole management team shares.

7

Case studies

7.1 INTRODUCTION

This chapter illustrates the report's themes and sheds light on how to avoid pitfalls commonly encountered in practice through eight case studies. We will briefly introduce them with reference to the Six 'I's model of Chapter 3.

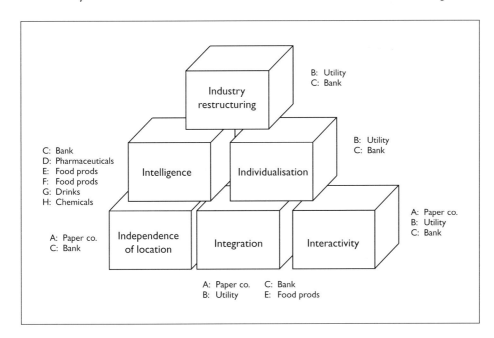

FIGURE 7.1

Case descriptions: building on integration

We begin with three cases which show how the six 'I's build on each other. In each of these cases, integration of customer data is a major theme. But integration is not an end in itself; rather, it is a cornerstone without which individualisation and an informed marketing strategy are impossible. This is diagrammatically illustrated in Figure 7.1, which shows which of the six 'I's are described in our case descriptions.

Case A describes some of the issues faced by a paper manufacturer that has traditionally been able to leave most of the marketing to its distributors. As it endeavours to support these distributors better, and to complement their sales efforts with services provided to the graphic designers who form important influencers, it needs to integrate its data about customers and influencers to support a smooth relationship between the location-independent media of telesales and direct mail, and the field salesforce.

A strong motivation for the moves towards integration in the utility of case B is to individualise the marketing of its services, if not the services themselves. Its marketing database has been useful for purposes such as mailing lists, but the utility now wishes to use it to tailor every customer interaction appropriately.

Industry restructuring is being forced on this utility through deregulation: IT is clearly critical in enabling the utility to service the new markets which this opens up, as well as providing a better service to its existing customers to improve retention. The bank of case C is in another industry facing massive restructuring, made possible by legislation which has broken down boundaries between such sectors as banks and building societies, and hastened by channel-based competition exemplified by First Direct. We describe its moves to offer a choice of channels – Internet, telephone and branch.

The remaining cases illustrate different approaches to the analysis of customer data once collected. Case D shows an example of a marketing planning system in a pharmaceuticals company. Another example of such a system is provided by case H. Case E shows the complementary approach of the executive information system (EIS), which unlike case D concentrates on hard sales data, the system's added value coming from its graphical display and from the different ways in which it can be aggregated. The third of the three approaches which we compared and contrasted in Chapter 6, causal modelling, is illustrated by cases F and G.

7.2 CASE A: CUSTOMER INFORMATION IN A PAPER COMPANY

Introduction

This case is interesting in that it shows the difficulty of gaining good customer information where distributors are between the organisation and its end users. It shows an organisation working towards better data collection, integration and distribution, and evolving its vision of how this information could be used in its marketing.

Company background

This large paper company produces a wide range of papers, distributing them multinationally, mostly through merchants. The part of the organisation studied produces speciality products such as high-quality letterhead paper. It has its own IT department.

Automation in sales and marketing

The IT director suggested that the use of IT was less mature within the sales and marketing functions than in manufacturing.

> In our shop floor manufacturing systems, I can show you detailed information about every quality defect on every roll of paper that was ever made over the past ten years. There are mountains of detailed data. But I think that I can say that sales and marketing are the most poorly served. We use computers for enquiries, quotations and order-taking. But it is all a bit disjointed – we are getting bits of benefit here and there but if we can bring it all together in a complete entity that has some structure, we would get more. We have lots of information lying about that we hardly ever touch.

The collection of better information is an issue, but not an end in itself:

> We need two elements for better sales and marketing systems. One is to gather data accurately and keep it clean. The other is to have a system that allows us proactively to do selling and marketing, using the information that we have captured.

Data collection issues

With several steps between the manufacturer and the end consumer, it can be difficult to acquire knowledge beyond the distributor. The company's market map is illustrated by Figure 7.2, which is annotated to show what information is held about different intermediaries in the chain to the consumer. As often in such cases, the level of detail decreases the further along the chain to the user you go. In the more co-operative relationship with distributors that is currently being developed, collecting better data together is regarded as an important building-block for becoming more proactive in the marketplace.

FIGURE 7.2

A paper manufacturer: market map

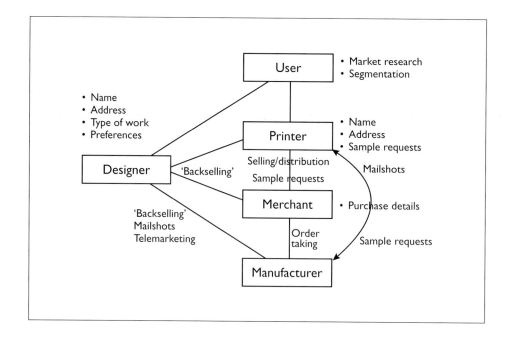

> We have a lot of data about what we already sell, which products move and which don't, who stocks which products and so on. We can take all of that to the kilo level, but we don't know what happens to it once it leaves the merchants – does it go to a smaller merchant? A printer? Directly to a consumer? As part of this new relationship, a joint team staffed by our people and the merchant's people is to help us get this information.

Information about printers has been built up from such sources as sample requests, leading to the capability to send mailshots and to telemarket. But the information captured is currently limited:

> There is some confusion about what is a lead. It could be a genuine enquiry from the print buyer of ICI, or a student ringing up asking, 'Have you got any nice yellow paper I could use for my research project?' We don't really differentiate between them because the systems we have just take names and addresses. So both are mailed with the same expensive packs.

A recent clean-up operation on one large mailing list more than paid for itself in the printing and mailing costs saved by deleting irrelevant or non-existent entries.

A good deal of effort has been expended in building relationships with the designers who act as important influencers, through a team of 'backsellers'. One request that has been made by sales to the IT director is to provide a simple system that captures some of the 'soft data' which this team comes across in its conversations with designers:

> a system which captures why people are buying or not buying, why did we lose that order, what is happening with competitors, what are their products and prices.

It does not necessarily follow, though, that the company should aim to be the prime repository of all this customer information. The marketing director was considering ownership issues:

> Do we hold this information and own it, or is it owned and kept inside the merchant but used by us?

The answer to this question was likely to vary with different types of information. The printers' main contact is with the merchants, who are the main source of information, samples and so on. So the use to which printer databases could be put was not clear-cut. With designers, however, 'we have more contact and the merchant views this as our job.'

Data integration, presentation and distribution

As well as collecting more information, various respects in which the information could be better integrated were raised. An example is tracking the link between enquiries, such as sample requests and future orders, so one could track what happened to the enquiry and, where appropriate, follow up to discover why it had not resulted in an order. Another example is integration across countries:

> We have databases in each European country – they are not linked and they are not consistent. When we analysed them we found there are three common fields between these eight databases. One is name, one is address and one is telephone number – terrific! We can get better consistency and a much better hit rate.

Presenting this integrated information as an aid to management decision making is also an issue, to provide, for example, graphs of sales in particular regions by distributor:

> At least we capture data at the UK level, but we don't have the systems to analyse it. The sales director can't at the press of a button find out whether sales are dropping off in the North of England. Or ask why that is so, and see that the competitors have just launched a product which is knocking us out, or they dropped their prices, or there is a promotion.

A data warehouse is currently being rolled out which addresses some of these issues.

As is often the case, though, integration seemed higher on the agenda of IT staff than of marketing colleagues, who were concerned with the commercial requirements driving change:

> Geographic standardisation of systems is irrelevant when the major issue is all about how we keep the data up to date. For example, how do you update when you are remote? Integration across countries is a future issue if a piece is designed in one country but printed in another.

Another simple case where the IT director had been asked to help with information dissemination was the product catalogue:

> By the time we've printed the product catalogue and issued it, it's out of date because the way we live is by innovation and niche markets. We are always stretching the product, and the brand. If we put it online, we will only need one copy of the product catalogue. When we update it everybody will have an updated copy.

The IT director regarded this system, valued by his sales colleagues, as a simple task technically that could be implemented within weeks using an Intranet, though he would need to address some concerns about security of sensitive information 'where anyone can download it'. From past experience in which projects with a prototype or early deliverable had gained approval over others with a conventional design–build cycle, he was pleased to have a small project with which he could build relationships:

> A prototype brings it out of the clouds and makes it real. Likewise, this system is low cost and low risk. I'd like to do everything yesterday, being impatient like most IT people. But I recognise that I can't. I still know that we can deliver a lot of value.

Involving IT in strategy formulation

This case has shown a company whose distributors have traditionally borne much of the brunt of front-line marketing. Hence it is at relatively early stages, compared with some of the other examples we have discussed, of the application of IT to marketing, with a focus on basic data collection and integration and simple uses such as producing mailshots with largely unsegmented mailing lists. How will the company move forward to use this information to 'proactively do selling and marketing' – and, indeed, should they? To complicate matters, the question is posed against a shifting business environment. The business faced, for example, the challenge of new, more direct channels such as office superstores:

> In these cases, the consumer is not influenced by a designer or printer and so this is a whole new game for us.

The IT director recognised that, whatever the answers, he would need to be actively involved in the more general debates where marketing strategy was formulated:

> It is all too easy to see IT as just a delivery mechanism, where the strategy for the business is already built. Now IT is getting more involved in strategy because I'm there and I'm trying to push it in, asking how can IT help us do this better? Some IT can fundamentally change the way you are going to run the business. It is that thought process which I am trying to bring to the organisation, at an early enough stage, when my colleagues are really theorising and blue-skying about different ways of doing business.

7.3 CASE B: EXPLOITING CUSTOMER DATA IN A UTILITY

Introduction

The last case showed some steps towards integrated customer data in a manufacturer which traditionally had been able to leave much of the marketing effort to its distributors. The utility in this case, although having to deal with large quantities of customer data for operational reasons such as billing, has also been partially shielded from the need to maximise their use for marketing purposes – not by distributors but by the lack of competition.

But like many utilities, this organisation is in an increasingly competitive environment, providing both new competitors for its traditional products and the opportunity to diversify itself. Both provide motivation for understanding its existing customers better, which has numerous IT implications. The company has for some time been endeavouring to shift from a product focus to a customer focus, with a relationship marketing group trying to ensure a unified approach to customer relationship management across the product-based organisation.

We describe how through integrated customer data the organisation hopes to enable a more individualised approach to its marketing, using segmentation and individual customer value assessment to target marketing initiatives and tailor the individual customer relationship.

Current situation

As in many organisations, the first step to a marketing database was to collect information from a variety of existing operational systems, hence creating what has been described by Sean Kelly as a 'first-generation data warehouse'. This is illustrated in Figure 7.3.

The operational systems centre around the core billing system for home consumption, which also provides a base for telephone enquiries. The information on customers – or, more correctly, on accounts – from this system is copied into the marketing database, where it is joined by information on the customer's purchases of related services and products from high street shops.

The resulting data can be used for such purposes as segmentation (supplementing the internal data with third-party information) and targeting, evaluating customers for direct mailing lists and estimating response rates. A segmentation based on attitudinal variables such as price, peace of mind, service and history has been developed.

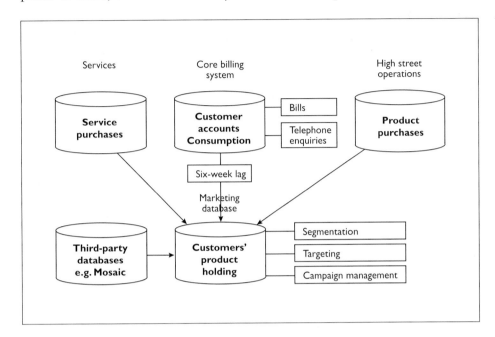

FIGURE 7.3

A utility's customer data: current situation

But problems include the time lag on getting information into this analysis database – up to six weeks depending on the information – and the limited capacity of the database for holding past history. The operational systems also differ in their view of the customer, making it difficult to gain an integrated view of the product holdings of one individual, or to track the individual when they move house:

We really record acounts. One unit might write to Dear Mr Ingram. Another might write to Dear John Ingram, and a third to Dear J Ingram, and we have no way of knowing what cross-postings are occurring. We need a common identifier of customers so that we can co-ordinate our campaigns. You won't get a bill one day and a leaflet to buy a new product the next day.

The lack of a clear view of customers also prevents calculation of the customer's lifetime value to the organisation:

> We are shifting from volumes of customers to understanding the value of the relationship. Depending on the differing value, one may be able, for example, to reduce effort and expenditure on those who cannot be of great value to us. The problem is that our current systems do not allow us to deliver that because we are organised by product. We primarily provide a commodity which people consume, and all our systems are designed around billing and handling queries relating to that.

Furthermore, the information flow into the marketing database is one-way. It is difficult to feed back knowledge gained about customers into the operational systems so as to affect such customer interactions as a customer's telephone call.

Future enhancements

A possible long-term vision being discussed is illustrated in Figure 7.4.

FIGURE 7.4

A utility: possible future

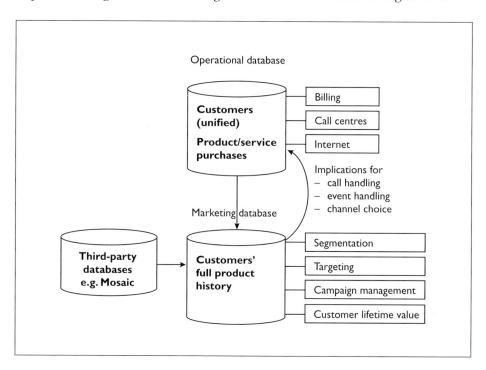

A more unified view of customers at the operational end – whether in practice from a single database or from a number of databases with common definitions – would enable the analysis database to look at the whole customer, including, for example, calculation of lifetime value.

> We will be able to create a better picture of lifetime value and drive some of our decisions on a return-on-investment basis – whereas we are currently driven by volumes of numbers rather than knowing values; we think in terms of 10 000 sales. We hope that this will improve our targeting and improve our response levels. So instead of sending out 100 000 pieces of direct mail we'll know we only have to send out 45 000, because we will be able to profile good respondents.

Another important feature sought is a feedback loop to the operational systems, to communicate issues such as likely channel preferences of the customer, implications for handling of an incoming call and appropriate proactive handling of events such as moving house.

> We need to be able to convey issues such as which segment a customer is in to customer service advisers at the call end. It is not just the information management, it is what do they do when they take the call.

This feedback loop is what characterises Sean Kelly's 'second generation' of data warehousing. Whether the analysis ('marketing') database and the operational database(s) are in practice separate is not the point, though it is likely to remain necessary to separate systems handling online transactions from those handling hefty analysis. A new operational generation could allow more freedom in the choice of the channel by which a customer is communicated with, such as the Internet – depending on the customer's preferences, as well as the individual picture of the customer built up.

> There are currently no differences between us and other suppliers. First Direct took a dull sector and shook it up. We need to think hard about channels. We will be able to profile likely respondents if we go onto the Internet as a channel to market. I think interactive digital TV is also likely to be of value to us here. The big issue is what is the curve for take-off? When will it really lift off?

7.4 CASE C: ADDING INTELLIGENCE TO CUSTOMER INTERACTION IN FINANCIAL SERVICES

Introduction

In the previous case, we saw how moves towards integrated customer information in a utility were motivated by a desire to treat customers individually and tailor all customer interactions accordingly. This case elaborates on this theme, describing a bank in which the operational systems have already been integrated with a unifying 'front-end' system which is currently being rolled out. Although in this respect perhaps one step ahead of the utility of the previous case, the bank is similarly grappling with how best to use this infrastructure to define the operational implications for analyses such as segmentation and customer value. In other words, how is the customer handled differently as a result of the knowledge gained about him or her?

With an inheritance including a merger between a bank and a building society, the organisation has a wide range of products available, including mortgages, bank accounts and credit cards, and high customer numbers. In using this asset base, it described its strategy several years ago as follows:

> We are in business to create long-term profitable relationships with our customers, by providing the full range of financial products supported by a unique bank.

What this emphasis on relationships means in practice was spelt out by a marketing manager.

> Fundamentally the difference between where we were, the transaction approach, and the relationship approach is that previously it was all about selling the product. Servicing it afterwards was regarded as a cost and an annoyance. You were focused down in the product silos, and you tended to treat every customer exactly the same, working on averages on all the customer/product and profit data. The relationship approach is to recognise that not all customers are created equal. They differ in what they are looking for, in the way

> they use the product and how they deliver stability to us through their buying behaviour. It means dealing in smaller segments, so we now ask which customers do we want to acquire, which give us a mix of short-term and long-term potential, and then which products should we focus on for that customer and which communication method is best, as well as how to retain them.

This strong theme of relationship management has numerous IT implications.

Integration of operational systems

The first piece of the IT strategy to support relationship management has been to integrate operational systems behind one common interface, providing a unified view of the customer to all staff.

> We are in the process of building a customer information system by taking extracts from all our product silos so we can build up a picture of our customer. We are trying to build into it contact management, so that anyone in any part of the organisation knows what's happened with that customer. We are also working towards the idea of being able to seamlessly transfer the customer from wherever they are actually speaking to a centre of excellence where staff can deal with their needs, as opposed to trying to multi-skill everywhere. The system opens windows of opportunity – branch staff know that we sent out a specific mailing in the past two weeks and can ask 'did you see our letter the other day?' It holds 20+ fields on every customer: you can set flags to show the propensity to buy a product and so on. Even if we can only deliver to a branch office some basic customer detail change information, that is a benefit because it saves accessing maybe ten databases.

This unified customer-facing system is illustrated on the left of Figure 7.5. The same information about customer product holdings and contacts is available to staff not only in branches, but also in call centres.

FIGURE 7.5

A bank: towards individualisation

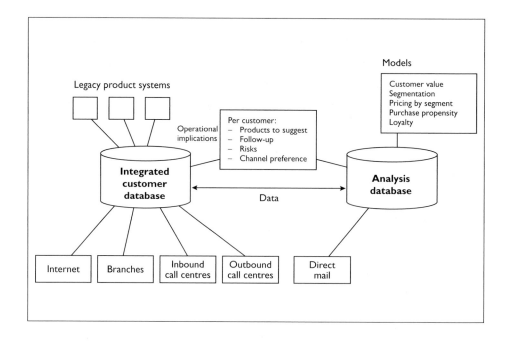

Analysis as a guide to operations

The second major component of the IT strategy is an analysis database. Originally developed in order to generate direct mail, this database also forms the basis for models which aim to understand the customer better, illustrated on the right of the figure. For example:

> There is a lot of work around purchase propensity, building models that say what is the customer's propensity to take out a mortgage and so on. The propensity modelling is sort of super-targeting, it is financing the future. Also attrition – what is the likelihood of losing a customer, and why – who are at high risk of leaving us?

This customer understanding is not just of use in generating direct mail. In a close parallel to the utility discussed in the previous case, the bank is now working out how analyses such as lifetime customer value should affect the handling of the individual customer interactions in the branch and on the telephone.

> We need a model which tells us the best approach to managing each relationship. At the moment we just smile and try to get customers to buy whatever they can possibly afford. We don't want them taking

money out of their savings to buy another product. So we are working on how we can make these decisions in time and correctly to let all parties benefit. Then the results need to be transferred to the customer information system and thence to the sales system in the branches. Deliver the decision back to the point of contact and allow the counter clerk to do something about it. Of course, there is always argument about where the decision should be made – at the point of sale, or do we do it all centrally?

A decision engine will take information and then offer the customer-specific decision, for example awareness that we should be contacting someone with a specific message using a known tone of voice. Another real issue is which channels should we be using to talk to them? We are trying now to select a decision engine. No one has got one, we are asking for proposals. It is called a request for miracles. But if it will do what we want, then we're in with a chance – because big banks either have to break themselves up and become a series of category killers or they are going to have to do this to survive.

Development into online banking, either through use of the Internet or interactive digital TV, is regarded as a natural extension to the approach:

There are many layers now but only one process to drive the system – that is our aim. We can simply plug in Internet banking but the security issues need to be done right.

These changes in the IT infrastructure were naturally being accompanied by far-reaching changes to the organisation. One was an evolution of the nature of the marketing department:

The department is in two. We have the luvvies and the wisies. The luvvies are in marketing communications and they come up with these posters and insets and eye-catching branch adverts. The wisies all have PCs on their desks, they talk about spatial mapping and they drive the analysis. They extract all the data and build models which let them look at current value, segment all customers and look at top/bottom segments. Realistically the marketing of the future is going to be full of wisies.

Overall, the strategy can be summarised as recapturing the individual service of the old-fashioned bank manager without the prohibitive costs entailed.

> In the real old days of bank managers banking was for the elite and 60 per cent of the population was unbanked. You trusted the bank manager because he'd look at your account and make recommendations. We plan to do the same. It might not be of financial value to us but we believe that in future it will be. It is all about current value of future income, isn't it?

7.5 CASE D: SUPPORTING R&D IN PHARMACEUTICALS

The attrition rate of new product developments in the pharmaceutical industry is high, development timescales are long and the R&D investment in a single product can be very large. Not surprisingly, the international marketing group of this pharmaceuticals multinational has changed its focus quite dramatically over the last few years, from concentrating on promotions and sales support for existing products, to spending much of its effort on providing a commercial input to research and development.

The R&D portfolio is overseen by a board-level new product development (NPD) committee, which holds a two-day review twice a year. Until recently, the committee comprised mainly senior technical staff. Then, in the recollection of the strategic planning manager:

> we were given a seat at the table. That put us on the spot a little bit. How should we represent our views? There was a whole raft of things that we wanted to summarise: the key issues, changing customers, of course, and the main issues in the therapy areas.

After some investigation, the marketing group decided the directional policy matrix (DPM) was the appropriate focus to their input to the committee.

Initially the use of the DPM was prototyped on paper, with basic software support using a spreadsheet. A consultant experienced in use of the DPM was enlisted to help to refine the methodology. The local company serving the largest market was closely involved in defining factors and weights. Scoring criteria were defined to standardise the scoring.

A software system was then developed to automate the use of the tool, performing calculations and displaying the matrix. The system also integrated this market-focused summary with various other charts providing technical and financial perspectives, providing an integrated portfolio planning system for the NPD committee. These included a 'development pipeline' chart of the projected release date of new products against their anticipated business strength; an R&D costing system to facilitate budgeting and control; a long-term forecast for existing and new products; and a chart summarising manufacturing risk under the two dimensions of the risks in successfully formulating the drug, and the risks involved in moving from the laboratory to bulk drug production. We briefly discussed this system earlier in this report: *see* Figure 4.4 illustrating the system.

After two and a half years of development and use, the marketing managers were in a position to reflect on the system's utility, aided by an internal survey of those in receipt of its outputs. One cited impact of the system was greater consensus. The strategic planning manager said:

> The portfolio review is more formalised in that we get transatlantic cross-functional teams together to put the final version in a form that we are happy with. The teams do their bit first. They come to a meeting with an agreed view so you don't get the usual internecine bickering.

But could this collection of data as an input to the DPM not be done equally well on paper?

> We did a Delphi for the factor weights. It was a successful way of gaining consensus and defending the weights that resulted. Factor scoring, however, is difficult without the benefit of a facilitator. For that, you really need something that's instant and online.

This perceived need was partly because the system made life easier for the facilitator:

> The beauty of that is that you do it once. I've done it on paper and it's tough – you come back with mounds of paper.

But it was also because, with software support, ideas were explored as they occurred, either before the meeting or during it, and managers would build confidence in the model as they saw how their views would influence the matrix.

Another perceived advantage of software support was in moving away from one-off planning towards the concept of a continuously updated marketing model of the new product portfolio. Whenever and wherever a planning exercise was held for a part of the portfolio, the updated data could be consolidated into the central system's database. Before each review, a snapshot would be taken, 'and then they can play with those data – it's an evolution'. This building of the model over time could also apply to qualitative data. Previously

> we were making decisions but we weren't recording how we made them or the assumptions behind them. Our corporate memory was zero.

The software prompted for 'real words on the system right there with all the data', to record the rationale for the numbers entered. The prompting for data resulted in data collection activities, which over time were improving the quality of the model. A market research manager reported that the company had joined a syndicated study collecting information on a range of disease areas as an input to the DPM.

The international marketing team had worked hard to obtain the commitment of the organisation's managers in its major countries through involving them in the development process and the data input. As well as the benefits that might be gained by the countries themselves, this was necessary in order to obtain good quality data – 'It's not the culture of this company to insist – and anyway you can't, truthfully.' An exception, in the view of one manager at least, was Japan, where 'the culture is such that if someone at HQ says we want you to do this, they do'. For providing inputs to the DPM, therefore, 'they were the first and most effective organisation'. The notion that the quality of Japanese input was less dependent on their conviction of the value of the exercise than that for other countries was not, however, corroborated by interviews with Japanese managers.

7.6 CASE E: MARKETING EIS IN A FOOD PRODUCTS COMPANY

Background

This food products company was the market leader in one product area in the UK with two major brands. Some parts of the product area were in long-term decline, and although the overall market size was still growing slightly, profitability was being squeezed. Although the product area could be divided into three or four sectors, cannibalisation was always an issue. With fairly homogeneous profit margins between products, the focus tended to be on volume to support the company's fixed costs, particularly in production capacity.

The company had a classical system of brand marketing, with product managers for each part of the product range under the brand reporting to a general manager responsible for the brand. Their responsibilities included drawing up annual marketing plans, co-ordinating pricing, promotions and new product development, monitoring performance against budget, and liaising with production and sales.

Voluminous amounts of information were needed to fulfil this role. Sales information was complemented by panel data, which provided market size and share estimates, and by store-based data. Before the computer system was introduced, the product managers were forced to spend large amounts of time analysing data. The general manager related an experience four years previously:

> I had to spend an inordinate amount of time – something in the order of two days – just to find out what our sales performance had been over the last decade on this particular product, to show that this business was in steady decline and that what they had been experiencing recently wasn't a blip or a skew. For me to spend two days just to get the data before you get the insight was absurd.

Inevitably, one result was that many analyses were not carried out. A product manager quoted an example:

> We didn't really understand when we saw a competitor introducing a new product what the impact was. Or if we did it was six months down the line rather than at an earlier stage when we could actually do something about it.

Introduction of the system

For the general manager, this experience was formative in commissioning a computer system.

> When I was involved in writing the proposal, it was all about saying of the three days it took to construct the board presentation on this, only one day was sitting down, thinking about it and mulling over the consequences. I'd much prefer that to be two days sitting, thinking and one day capturing the data.

A further motivation was to ensure value for money in promotional spending – here expressed by a product manager:

> We were spending a huge amount on promotions and no one really knew if they were making any money nor how much ... Things are getting more and more complicated and if we don't understand what is going on, then we haven't a hope.

After an IT manager had co-ordinated the requirements from different departments and surveyed the available systems, an executive information system, IRI DataServer (reviewed in McDonald, Wilson and Hewson, 1996), was purchased and tailored to the company's needs. It included hierarchies of products, customers and time periods, and allowed sales to be viewed by any combination of account, product, depot and time. It also included consumer panel data. Information could be obtained graphically or in tabulated form, either on the screen or in paper reports. Extensive facilities were available for selecting the information required, and then viewing further data in order to explore phenomena of interest. For example, one could pick out some products from a sector and drill into those products by account; or one could compare all the products introduced in the last three years against those that were introduced in the last ten years. The system is diagrammatically illustrated in Figure 4.3.

Terminals were available for all the product managers, who received a degree of training – though perhaps not enough.

> We sat down for a couple of hours and tried to understand what was on the system and how to use it. I don't think people really got the training that they needed. There are still several people in the department who don't know how to manipulate the data within the system. They know how to turn it on and how to call up a few reports that they set up in the past. But there are a lot of people who still struggle to actually manipulate it. The system is very easy. But you've got to know a few little tricks and a few short cuts. And you need to understand how the markets and accounts are structured.

System usage, as a result, seemed somewhat dependent on computer experience and confidence.

Impacts of the system

All the product managers, however, relied on the system extensively, both for reporting and for ad hoc analyses. One, who by his own admission was as yet 'desperately slow' on the system, related how previously

> you couldn't easily add it up by groups, nor could you drill down by account ... Products are babies. If you don't look after them, they will die. So you need to be on top of it in terms of facts, figures, and what the accounts are doing.

The system was consistently perceived as having achieved the objective of providing faster access to data.

> They only have to spend a small amount of time at the terminal getting some data. Clearly there is easy access to insight, whereas previously that was impossible. It was literally a case of calculator, pen and paper or some Lotus spreadsheet where you had to key in the data.

Could the objective have been achieved by employing clerical staff to manipulate the data? The general manager thought not. As a product manager looked at one piece of information, that would suggest another to look at: the search could not be specified in advance.

> If you had a clerical person sitting here, clearly because it's an iterative process they're not going to take that piece of learning and modify their investigation from there on, whereas a product manager attuned to the business issue is going to respond to that latest piece of learning.

One cited impact of the greater speed of analysis was the carrying out of more analyses – for example, how advertising had performed, what the impact of a competitive move had been, or the effectiveness of a promotion.

> Because it was so difficult and people were so rushed, nobody even attempted to do it. And therefore, we didn't really understand to the degree that we understand now – and we can still improve that – how efficient our promotional spend was.

As a result, decisions were better rather than necessarily faster:

> Somebody would come up with a promotional idea and say we can get six times uplift. So we'd order packaging for six times uplift. We're now in a position where we can say did we really get six times uplift the last time we did it? Why and in which accounts? How much space in store did we get for the promotion? And it starts to allow us to be more objective and to take better decisions because we are dealing with real information rather than just people's views on what happened. I do think it's helped with the quality of decision making. In terms of speed, I think it's helped because it's slowed things down. People now say rather than 'let's run away and do the promotion again', 'let's sit back and analyse it'.

One product manager talked in terms of the power that the extra access to information had provided, both for internal and external dealings. He quoted an example:

> We can say to Tesco's, your promotion last month gave you six times uplift. Shouldn't we be doing it again?

Other examples were to chase account managers if a product was below target in an account and to provide feedback to the factory.

As well as these tactical uses, the system was felt to be providing data for planning purposes. Moving annual totals were used to look at longer-term trends to remove some of the volatility from promotions:

> When you've got this sort of volatility it hides the actual trend. You can't see where it's going. You do an MAT on it and all of a sudden you can see the turning points and the actual trends.

System restrictions and complementary systems

Some restrictions reduced the system's utility for planning, however. First, the absence of online promotional data led to difficulties in understanding the past as a basis for predicting the future:

> We have promotional planners but they don't tend to be filed well – so if you're looking back in time it's difficult to find out what went on – nor particularly accurate. You'll find one and the dates won't correspond to the weeks you've had the uplift because something's changed and no one's updated the plan.

Second, in the absence of econometric modelling facilities, forecasts could only take account of the effect of promotions in a judgemental way. The general manager planned to change this (*see* Figure 7.6):

We're going to have to get into a tool that's able to grab data from a previous promotional activity and study how these elements had been behaving previously. Through this kind of replication and if you replicate those in the future, you will get a performance range that can be used for forecasting. And it's that modelling of behaviour which we don't have. And we don't at this stage have the human or the software capability to capture that. This software is looking to do that.

FIGURE 7.6

Marketing data usage in a food products company

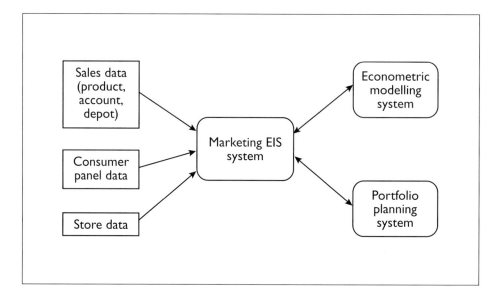

This was not, however, expected to be easy, as promotions included difficult-to-quantify aspects such as the degree of support given to the promotion by the store in how the product was placed on the shelf.

Other problems with planning concerned organisational procedures. The assumptions underlying forecasts were not felt to be adequately recorded, while the short time period in which budgets were set restricted the extent to which analyses could be carried out on the system to ensure that the budgets were appropriate. The result, in the view of some product managers, was that the commitment to budgets was lower than it might be.

The general manager perceived the need to complement the system with portfolio analysis to help with overall strategy – though he anticipated that this would be used by himself rather than the product managers. Although there was a considerable degree of consumer switching between parts of the portfolio,

> we try and portfolio manage when we can, by focusing for example on meal-time occasions ... that is very different from something like a snack ... One element of my job is managing the mix – swinging the mix towards more profitable products is clearly an issue.

He had recently obtained a simple portfolio matrix package, Portfolio Manager (reviewed in McDonald, Wilson and Hewson, 1996), though it had not yet been used. He intended to feed data from the system into the package.

> I'm looking to embrace portfolio management in the day-to-day process of planning by taking the burden off the individual. The big concern of portfolio management is that you get a series of data that is then presented inaccurately – particularly if you're doing a BCG or something like that. People do it by getting a 5, 10 and 50p coin out of their pocket – and, God forbid, people draw conclusions on that. At the end of the day just about any business does it to some level – sometimes on the back of a fag packet, sometimes more astutely, and I'm trying to take it to an area where at least it's accurate.

7.7 CASE F: CAUSAL MODELLING IN A FOOD CONGLOMERATE

Background

This case illustrates causal, or econometric, modelling, which was explained in sections 3.5 and 4.8: *see* Figure 3.7 for an example of this technique.

This food conglomerate had been built up by a series of acquisitions over the last decade. Ranging from drinks to chocolate, its European business now had a business unit per country 'managed with a frightening degree of autonomy'. In many respects the culture inevitably was not fully unified, given the diverse historical strands: 'We are working in a culture which isn't quite a culture yet, it's still 30 or 40 different cultures.'

The planning process was one mechanism that the European and world headquarters staff had to unify the diverse approaches and to enable review across business units. A unified format of annual plans included forecasts of the market, the company's share and profit, with associated marketing plans for achieving them.

One area in which business units were claimed to differ was in the approach to marketing information. In the United States, econometric modelling was reportedly deeply embedded:

> When a marketing manager is presenting, he may also have to present modelling proof – not just 'in order to get at that share I need this price gap', he will also need, somewhere in the appendix, the modelling that's gone into that.

The European vice-president responsible for marketing information wished to build up similar expertise in Europe. This was not a trivial exercise:

> We need not just the capability to produce the stuff, we need educated management to ask for it and know what to look for.

He therefore appointed a modelling expert to be the champion for modelling in Europe, providing assistance in modelling to the countries, and building up their own expertise. The champion explained the difficulties of the task:

> They tend not to have specialists – some of them don't have research departments, let alone modelling specialists within them. That means we have to have a network, and we have to improve the capability of anyone who is capable of modelling. We have enough experience to know that, with modelling, a little knowledge isn't just dangerous, it's fatal. So we try to keep the modelling in the hands of those who we halfway trust.

Purchase and use of system

It would take time, however, to build up the modelling skills in each country, so for the time being there was a bottleneck. The champion looked for a computer system that would help to ease this.

> Whatever system you choose has got to give great productivity gains to those rare animals that you're entrusting to it. The need is to very quickly be able to find the limits of the information in a dataset.

This implied simplicity rather than richness of facilities: 'The real productivity savings come from stopping them wasting their time for another week.' It also implied graphical presentation: 'If the software brings with it some reasonable graphics, you can almost see the thing working.'

Another factor in the choice was to allow non-linear relationships to be modelled. A neural-network-based modelling package, 4Thought, met both criteria. But were non-linear relationships not harder for managers to understand than traditional linear regression?

> People are quite relaxed about shapes of curves. They can see that as you get close to some barrier price the continuity will break, that there will be a point beyond which the damage will be done. People can get their minds around that, and they can get their minds round something that comes back and presents them with response curves and things like that.

To date, the main purpose of the system was to model the factors driving market size and share in key markets in order to inform decisions on changes to the marketing mix. The secondary purpose was forecasting on the basis of the model, though 'we haven't started from forecasting as the primary role – we have started from understanding the primary levers'. The champion would assist a country with building models in some important markets and work towards a situation where the country could continue unaided itself.

> I have a missionary role, to get the business units to believe so much in the importance of modelling that they spend some headcount on it.

Several countries had so far recruited their own modelling person.

Some aspects of modelling he found were best tackled by a different approach. Structural modelling to determine the best definitions of market segments was achieved using a separate methodology. Following this, the 4Thought system could be used on the resulting market segments.

Example of use

In one particular country, the company was the market leader in one category. Its main umbrella brand had a premium sub-brand P, and a second sub-brand which was positioned as a healthier alternative, H. The H brand was priced higher than the premium brand, and its sales had withered since its launch three years previously. The business choices included cutting its price, increasing its advertising and replacing it with a line extension to the premium brand.

The modelling champion was called in to help to model the market share of H. He set up a model with weekly data drawn from a consumer panel going back a number of years, with an alternative model based on monthly data – the basis on which media data were available. The variables included promotions, the average price of H, its price gap with P, its price gap with various competitors, media spend and seasonality – unexpectedly a significant factor in the share model, probably due to promotions patterns of the various competitors who promoted heavily at certain times of the year.

This resulted in a curve that showed what the share of H would be on various pricing strategies, showing a relatively modest share gain if the price of H was lowered to that of P. It also showed that the effect of some complementary advertising would be to halve the price cut required to achieve a given share. A further pattern thrown up accidentally was that promotions were occurring when H was priced high rather than being used to highlight a low price.

One thing the model could not do was model the effect of price cuts on competitors' prices. This was modelled using a separate methodology and separate software support.

The champion's resulting report to the country managers still left a number of decisions to be taken.

> It leaves them with all the choices. Then they will tell me what they have decided to do. That's fine. What we have given them is the means of making a smarter decision than letting the loudest-mouthed product manager win.

The model was also left behind for the country managers to use for forecasting purposes, and to provide a continuous check on whether the factors driving the market were remaining the same.

> I loaded them up a much simpler model for forecasting their market. They are doing their business plan for next year. They need to be able to predict in simple terms ... I have instructed them to ring if the actual is outside the error margin by a factor of 3 or more. Models don't break, the reality walks away from them, and you need to find out when that is as quickly as possible and work out why.

Choosing when to apply the system

Company culture

In some cases, data were not available to build econometric models. The company culture did not appear to support the use of judgemental alternatives such as portfolio matrices.

> Our company culture would reject that. If we didn't have the data, our next step would be survey, through the brand price trade-off methodology. Failing that, we would say to some guy, make a decision. If this was a minor brand where the risk to the business was fairly small, we'd say let's just do it. If it's wrong maybe we can rescue it next year. The interesting thing is to compare ourselves with [x], who are our biggest global competitor. We will go modelling first, survey next, make a bloody decision. [x], we think, goes decision, if any doubt do a survey, and what's all this modelling nonsense?

Level of applicability

Modelling had so far been used within categories rather than for cross-category resource allocation at corporate level. This was not just due to the technical difficulties involved: political and organisational considerations were also seen to be relevant.

> We are trying in the States to do cross-category portfolio work. You can optimise your spend within a category. If I had a million dollars for a category, I would know how to spend it. So in theory we could add them all up and say, 'Which of you guys is going to get this million?' You have to recognise that you can starve a category if you let the arithmetic go wild ... The guy in European head office might say 'it seems to us you shouldn't have more than the following in funds, and we're going to give it to this country'. Now that's politically an enormous step.

Match with intuition

To what extent were the system's outputs accepted only when they were concordant with the managers' intuition?

> Many of our clients are cherry-pickers. If we do a body of modelling that's close enough to what they were thinking, they are off and running with it. If we do something that they're uncomfortable with, it will become an ongoing discussion point. We say if a modelling conclusion looks wrong, there's a good chance it is.

7.8 CASE G: CAUSAL MODELLING IN A DRINKS COMPANY

Background

This drinks company regarded itself as brand led. The industry was

> increasingly polarising around big brands. It's important to be able to go into an account with a big portfolio, with the big brands and heavyweight support behind them.

A marketing manager admitted that this emphasis had slipped for a while following supply and invoicing problems which accompanied a takeover: 'We were certainly sales led, in a desperate attempt to minimise losses through the disruption to customers.' The emphasis had now returned to building brands, however. The importance of marketing had been heightened further by legislative changes which had the effect of freeing up the market.

The marketing director had several teams: brand management, market research, market planning, commercial and PR. Market planning acted as a facilitator and information provider to the brand managers in the production of their annual brand plans, providing market forecasts, competitor research and ad hoc analyses such as assessment of promotion effectiveness. Their role complemented the market research team which commissioned consumer research.

Econometric modelling was used for the ad hoc analyses in order to model the factors driving market share for a particular product, on the basis of historical time series data, as a basis for decisions about the marketing mix.

Purchase and use of the system

The 4Thought system was purchased for use on such ad hoc analyses. As well as market share or size models, it was hoped that the system would make possible profiling applications, where in place of a time series, the data varied by some other variable. For example, the marketing planning manager tried an analysis of which outlets would be likely to succeed with a certain product. This particular exercise proved impracticable due to inadequate data on the company's database, and use of the system so far had been restricted to time series work, though various such profiling applications were being considered.

The 4Thought system was chosen largely because of the simplicity of its user interface, rather than because of its neural network technology.

> If I can get at a forecast that I'm happy with, that's enough, and I want to be able to arrive at that forecast easily. I have not seen a regression package packaged in the same way as this is. If I did, there might be a lot more people making good use of regression.

Previously, a regression extension to a standard PC spreadsheet package had been used.

> This is the first system I have seen that really lets you move the data around easily. At the time I was using something called Lotus Regression, which was really difficult to move your data in and out of.

Nevertheless, there was one perceived advantage of neural networks: 'Neural networks allow us to look at curvilinear relationships. That's an attraction.' While non-linear models could be built with regression, 'I think that neural networks handle it much more readily.'

Example of use: price sensitivity of a major brand

One exercise conducted with the system involved analysis of the price sensitivity of one of the company's major brands. Using information from grocery retailers, the model tracked the drivers of weekly market share over the last few years, with variables including brand price, brand price for various competitors, display distribution (tracking posters about the product) and product distribution. The choice of competitors was based on the company's market hierarchy, which was determined separately, and allocated the product to a mainstream rather than a premium segment. General media spend did not need to be included as the model was good without it, accounting for 94 per cent of the variance in market share, over a period when the products share varied from 2 per cent to 20 per cent.

The model was then used to test out various pricing scenarios. Conclusions were reached about the optimal level of pricing in terms of profit: it was found that a price just below the competitor average would improve profitability. Scenarios were also tested about the timing of promotions. One manager had suspected that promotions should be timed when competitors were not promoting rather than at the same time, as at present. The model showed, however, that the current approach was the right one. A final conclusion was that it would not be possible to return to the market share previously achieved, as had been hoped.

Using the model's outputs about pricing proved difficult, however. In order to act on the model's conclusions, information on competitors' future prices was necessary.

> It's great that we have an understanding of what's affected it in the past, but unless we can accurately model the future of those components, there's a restriction. And at the moment we haven't accurately modelled the future.

The marketing planning manager related this to the resource available for this modelling work.

> This came about because I decided to be proactive, staying late after work to get it done. I am going to have to get a budget signed off to make sure we can get hold of that data.

In the meantime, could the pricing conclusions not be used tactically, reacting to competitors' prices as they occurred? There were various barriers to this. First, tactical decisions relied on the salesforce, who needed to be convinced of the model's correctness. In the view of a marketing manager serving the salesforce:

> The easiest people to convince are analysts. The problem is convincing the rest of the organisation, particularly salespeople, who aren't interested in all this fancy stuff. And therefore one needs to be able to get back into the data in a very simple way and say, look guys, here are the patterns.

Second, pricing and promotional decisions were largely allocated at the start of the year. Third, salesforce decisions were taken at store level rather than the aggregated level used in the model. On the promotions findings, however, the marketing manager agreed that the model had proved of value: 'Something very practical there – I can say, guys, this is the time when we ought to be promoting.'

The applicability of econometric modelling

A more fundamental difficulty was raised by two interviewees. The model, like much of the thinking in the company and the industry, was based on a market hierarchy which separated the standard drinks from premium drinks and one category of drinks from another. In their view, these distinctions were artificial, and shown to be false by consumer data which illustrated that many people switched from one category to another.

> It's production speak. If you explore consumer data, you find that the areas aren't so much grey as they don't exist.

This could, in their view, have profound implications for pricing and other aspects of marketing. The econometric modelling could only to a limited extent help to validate these ideas – if the price of a competitor supposedly in a different segment was found to be a significant variable, that would suggest that the segment boundaries were incorrectly drawn, or at least were not hard and fast.

For one of the interviewees, this illustrated the general principle that multiple sources of market information, and multiple systems analysing it, needed to be used to complement each other.

> There are three approaches. There's a descriptive technique, which is to study the data; there's consumer research, not so much the ad hoc but the continuous stuff, where you can identify the consumer relationships, the behavioural patterns that the consumer has; and then you apply what you know in this sort of statistical data, and you know from the quality of the statistics produced whether the pattern that you're trying to explore is robust or not. I see them as complementary along a range.

So what was the role of judgemental models within the company? Models such as the DPM would certainly not be appropriate if based on consensus, according to one marketing manager, because the conventional wisdom was so pervasive:

> That's what this market operates on – and it's a bloody disaster. Because they are convinced that the market works in a certain way.

As communication devices, however, they might have a role in providing graphical presentations of data.

7.9 CASE H: PLANNING IN A SPECIALITY CHEMICALS COMPANY

Background

This speciality chemicals company had grown from a small company serving the textile industry after the war to a profitable diversified company with a £350 m turnover, selling into a number of industries around the world. The UK still provided 60 per cent of the manufacturing, but only 12 per cent of turnover, the rest being provided by a series of subsidiaries and agents. With a reasonably dominant position in its markets, it had shown high growth in recent years. The board reportedly felt this growth could probably be maintained through geographical expansion into parts of the world in which it currently did little business, but was well aware that this presented a number of organisational development issues.

With this in mind, it had recently appointed a group strategic planning manager, reporting to the group CEO. One identified weakness on which he was working was the lack of marketing processes. Marketing activities were carried out on an ad hoc basis by sales managers, and R&D expenditure tended to be a 'bunfight' between divisions. He claimed to be putting into place processes for forecasting, market intelligence, annual planning and control. He also had involvement in choosing strategy and delivering aspects of the strategy on a project basis.

History of use: evaluating a new business opportunity

The system was bought to look at one particular issue of choice of strategy, on which the strategic planning manager was called in to provide an independent assessment. His understanding was that one of the group executives was very keen to move to a particular business area, but that the others were unconvinced, feeling it did not relate very well to the other parts of the business.

He decided to try the Business Insight system to assist with the assessment. He interviewed a number of board members and other relevant managers in order to obtain the necessary input, translating the system's prompts into questions and feeding the answers into the system. He then wrote an assessment for the board, backing up some of his 'fairly subjective conclusions' with appendices containing printouts from the system.

He presented his report to the board, and used the system to answer some of the questions that arose in discussion. The board decided not to proceed with the new business area.

System description

Based on an integration of marketing and strategy theory such as portfolio analysis, and Porter's five-forces model and generic strategies, the system provides a detailed analysis of a particular product market or business unit. Unlike the multiple product-market systems, it examines one product market in depth rather than assisting directly with issues of portfolio balance and resource allocation, although principles about these issues are raised as they might affect the product market in question.

The system prompts for a number of inputs covering all aspects of business strategy, including the nature of the product, the market and the competition, the company's human resources, marketing and sales, production issues and financial information.

It then produces a number of strategy charts, such as a chart assessing the product market's match with Porter's generic strategies of cost leadership, differentiation and focus, and a product positioning matrix plotting price against value. These are complemented by advice of various kinds, including a strengths/weaknesses analysis and an assessment of the product market on key factors such as profit potential. The reasons for advice given can be traced back in terms of the inputs that led to the advice and how they were combined.

Impacts of the system

The system was used not just to produce recommendations, but also to debate them. This had some advantages over a paper report, in the strategic planning manager's view:

> We had it up on a screen as we were talking through the results. And people could say, I don't agree with that, I think you've completely underestimated the importance of having a distributed, well-trained salesforce able to respond in half an hour, and that's how we defined responsiveness to customers' requests, and you've completely underestimated how good we are at that. And you'd say, OK, well

> let's see, and change the scoring, and see what happened to the overall rating of attractiveness or whatever. And of course, by and large, small changes in one thing don't have much effect. There are some exceptions to that. So it was a kind of a way of saying, we might be wrong about that individual thing, but unless you can point out a series of things we're wrong about, it doesn't change the overall conclusion. So it was a way of giving a weighting to individual issues which could be instantaneously reflected in an overall conclusion.

Inevitably, an issue in such discussions was the weight that could be attached to the system's extensive advice:

> You always then get onto the next issue, which was how exactly is this black box combining all these various factors? And of course I can't answer that because I don't know. All I can say is, based on my experience of doing these things before, I'm not really surprised at the way in which it combines the answers – all it is really is Porter's five forces plus a bit more in a fancy slide show. It's in line with what I would have expected. You're right that I can't explain what the weighting is – if you want we can go back and alter the weighting. For the purpose I was prepared to trust it.

How about the argument that the advice was trying to quantify the unquantifiable with excessive precision?

> I'm an engineer. My approach is always that you can never have enough numbers. But I think it's particularly true here, because on the pendulum between gut feel and tell me the numbers we're off scale on the gut feel end. So I don't have any problem with asking for numbers here, because we've got far too few.

But if the system was trusted because its outputs matched expectations, was it simply confirming what managers already thought? For the strategic planning manager, the answer was no:

> You get a list of twenty key issues. I would have said four or five of them were not obvious but were probably right.

It appeared to confirm the thinking of some of the other managers present:

> Some of the non-executive directors were involved as well – it probably confirmed some of the concerns that someone who's a bit more detached would have. They are unbiased, relatively, so an unbiased collation, which is what it was, more or less reflected what they expected.

For example, the system's generic strategies analysis found that there was no single clear strategy, with arguments between cost leadership and differentiation finely balanced. This led to the argument that the company was already competing in enough areas on the basis of cost leadership, and this area would rapidly become very dependent on low cost. The system had not changed the mind of the champion of the new business area, however.

> He couldn't knock down the basis for the conclusion on an individual basis. But it's a bit like which football team do you support – they aren't susceptible to complete rationalisation, are they, sometimes? And there's always a balance of this hard stuff with judgement and gut feel and so forth. All that you could point out was that there was weight of evidence for a guilty verdict. You couldn't actually be the jury.

Had the system had any educational side-effects to help the strategic planning manager in his missionary role?

> Well, it's a kind of condensed MBA strategy class, isn't it? I'm not sure you can learn very much from it if you haven't been through it before. Or if you haven't read a book about the five forces and all the rest of it. I think you need lots of examples of what is meant by a lot of these concepts. And it doesn't give any examples, because it's trying to use your data as an example. And it's not really, to me, a

> tool that is a good first approach to the subject. You've got to know the rules of the game first, and then you can use it as an assistant, to collate their answers and present them back quickly. That's what it's good at.

In summary, in the view of its champion, the system had helped to provide a focused debate that resulted in a clear-cut decision.

> It put a line in the sand. It allowed you to do an exercise, capture the opinions, make a decision, and rule further discussion out of court. So probably what would have happened is we wouldn't have made as clear a decision as quickly.

Success factors

In the strategic planning manager's view, at least, the value of the tool was in analyses of new business areas or radical changes of strategy, where the board did not have sufficient expertise to take decisions unaided. In accordance with this view, the system had not been used for a decision on a divestment, which had focused on short-term financial problems.

> Most of our decisions are about how to improve what we now do, and the rate of expansion of the manufacturing, and the marketing and distribution scope. That's what we spend most of our time discussing. There, I don't think this thing would be as applicable. It's applicable if there is much less information, and there's less knowledge and experience of the business area. The value of that thing was that it was a way of condensing a new area and comparing it with something that was existing.

The system had been applied with the strategic planning manager acting as a facilitator. What would have happened without the facilitator could only be answered hypothetically.

> The system kind of puts another person into the room. The person is a kind of robot. It was up to me to run the robot and explain what the robot was saying in language they understood. I guess if they had sat there and thrashed the keyboard they wouldn't have taken much notice of it.

One further requirement for use was adequate time to feed in considerable quantities of data and to research them as necessary.

> It's pretty heavy on data input. The balance to that is you can get something out without putting very much in. But to get something out that was recognisable it was pretty input-intensive. But that's the way of the world – you get out what you put in – I don't think one should be too surprised at that. But the fact of the matter is it took a long while.

8

Conclusions: the need for further research

8.1 THE MOTIVATION FOR RESEARCH

In this report, we have presented our findings to date in this domain. We now turn to the future, to ask what further research is needed. We asked a number of practitioners that question, and we will turn to their answers below. But first, some comments from our expert respondents are instructive. The need for rigorous research into what benefits are achieved in practice was pointed out by a number of respondents:

> Too many projects are IT driven rather than business driven, and the focus is on achieving data integration and an elegant architecture, rather than developing the application vision to drive out real business advantage.
>
> Sean Kelly

> The IS/IT literature is very weak on benefits. There is quite a lot of anecdotal, pseudo-case information. There is very little specifically on IT in marketing. What there is, is anecdotal.
>
> Professor John Ward

A particular issue is the motivation for research. Several interviewees emphasised the importance of research that is independent of particular supply-side interests:

> There is a widespread belief that spending £5 m on a service system will make your customers happier people, and yet if you look for research that supports that view there's virtually none. It's very odd, until you realise that there's this huge IT industry that has an interest in selling these things. A lot of the research tends to focus on application package suppliers – in particular, on quite small suppliers of packaged contact management software. It discovers that collectively the whole lot probably don't turn over more than £100 million in the UK; that most people that buy from them aren't terribly satisfied; and yet there are these claims of these astonishingly large benefits. No one ever, to my knowledge, has done a proper

tracking study to see if they got those benefits. If you talk to consultants in the area, they will say, 'Sooner or later we will get to a point where we are more honest about that, but the suppliers are breathing down our necks and wouldn't like it if we didn't present a rosy picture.'

Professor Robert Shaw

Benefits are a terrible subject not just for paucity of research, but also for motivation of research.

Professor Kit Grindley

8.2 THE PRACTITIONER PERSPECTIVE

A scoping matrix

At a workshop held at Cranfield in May 1998, participants from a number of companies were asked to complete a matrix of possible research areas, given below, in order to guide the formulation of research objectives for future research. The rows represent areas of the application of IT to marketing, while the columns show some different aims that the research might have. The consolidated input of the participants is shown in Figure 8.1. The stars indicate the number of participants who considered the cell an important area for research. Some clusters have been highlighted to show where a measure of consensus was reached by participants.

FIGURE 8.1

The need for research – a scoping matrix

Area of application \ Research aim	Mapping available technologies/ applications	Benefits obtained in practice	Success factors for achieving benefits	Process for integrating with marketing strategy
Task support for sales and marketing operations at the customer interface	*** 1	****** 2	***** 3	****** 4
Integrated sales and marketing management information	5	** 6	** 7	* 8
Generating market knowledge with market research/data warehousing	** 9	* 10	11	12
Task/group support for management decision making	* 13	* 14	* 15	* 16
Electronic commerce, e.g. Internet, interactive TV, EDI, WAN	*** 17	** 18	19	**** 20
Information as integral part of product/service offering	* 21	* 22	* 23	**** 24

Rows of the matrix

A simplified typology of application areas was used as follows:

1. *task support for sales and marketing operations* – the systems based on customer databases encompassing channels such as the salesforce ('salesforce automation'), direct mail, the telephone ('call centres' or 'telemarketing') and the Internet;

2. *integrated sales/marketing management information* – whereby IT can present integrated information on customers, products and transactions for purposes such as control against plan and campaign management;

3. *generating market knowledge through integrating market research and data warehousing concepts* – as exemplified by causal modelling for price/promotions decisions, and undirected data mining for previously unrecognised segments or buying patterns;

4. *task/group support for sales/marketing management decision making* – for example, marketing planning group decision-support tools that support a cross-functional board-level planning exercise, illustrated by cases D and H;

5. *electronic commerce* – complementing traditional routes to market with channels such as the Internet and interactive TV;

6. *information as an integral part of the product/service offering* – providing information-based products and services electronically, e.g. over the Internet.

Columns of the matrix

Using the six application areas outlined above, it was suggested that under each application area, research might have four possible broad aims. These were:

1. mapping available technologies/applications in order to demonstrate their potential to contribute to the marketing tasks of organisations;

2. researching benefits obtained in practice;

3. establishing success factors for achieving benefits;

4. establishing processes for integrating IT requirements with marketing strategy.

Research objective and questions

From the responses to this matrix, it is evident that key concerns of practitioners relate to row 1 (*Task support for sales and marketing operations at the customer interface*) and column 4 (*Process for integrating with marketing strategy*). Thus the central objective which we propose for further research is:

> To explore what process organisations can follow in order to integrate decisions on information systems support for sales and marketing operations with the organisation's marketing strategy.

We use 'information systems' rather than 'information technology' as our concern is with the function of systems and use of information rather than the technical means by which this is achieved. By 'marketing' we mean the marketing process – that of matching the customer's needs or wants to the capabilities of the organisation – rather than simply the marketing department, which may perform only part of this wider role.

The following questions arise from this research objective:

Question 1 (derived from box 1 in Figure 8.1)

How can marketing activities be mapped so as to distinguish the different systems that can support them?

Information systems supporting sales and marketing operations may vary widely in their nature and effects. In order to provide a basis for distinguishing between these, a map of the possible technologies and the marketing tasks they are supporting is needed (column 1). We presented an initial version of such a map in Chapter 4. A map showing the relationship between technology and marketing activities can help to make marketers aware of the potential of information technology to enhance marketing effectiveness.

Question 2 (derived from box 2 in Figure 8.1)

What are the benefits, in terms of the contribution to the organisation's marketing strategy, of systems supporting marketing operations?

Having developed a map of IT in marketing, the issue of system benefits and, indeed, disbenefits – unintended negative effects of systems – needs to be addressed (column 2 of the scoping matrix). Areas of potential benefit which need to be studied include: improved methods of customer segmentation;

differentiation through IS/IT-enabled channels; and relationship marketing through IT support throughout the customer lifecycle. We believe that Cranfield's Benefits Dependency Network (Figure 8.2) is a valuable tool for researching benefits.

Question 3 (derived from box 3 in Figure 8.1)

What success factors relating to the design, implementation and use of systems determine whether benefits are achieved?

Prior research has revealed that the success of information systems is dependent on many factors which are not directly related to the use of the technology. These include organisational culture, senior management support or championship of new ways of working, management of change and reskilling of staff, to name just a few. As yet there is little evidence which specifically guides marketing managers in this respect, an exception being the research into software for marketing planning reported in Chapter 6.

Question 4 (derived from boxes 4, 20 and 24 in Figure 8.1)

What changes in industry processes and relationships are occurring, and can be expected to occur, as a result of IT-enabled marketing?

As we have seen, the application of technological advances to marketing can radically change the structure of industries. Such changes include the decimation of intermediaries such as high-street car insurance brokers, their replacement by new intermediaries and influencers such as telephone brokers or the Internet that will find the best quote for car insurance, and the emergence in previously undifferentiated sectors of niche operators targeting specific segments derived from geodemographic systems. It is hoped that research might throw light on how future changes to industry structure, such as the speculations on the car retailing industry in Figure 8.3, might be predicted.

Question 5 (derived from box 4 in Figure 8.1)

How do organisations need to adapt their marketing planning processes in order to ensure that the potential for IT applications to contribute to marketing strategy is fully exploited?

Once the potential benefits of systems are understood, companies will be in a better position to decide where systems can contribute to marketing strategy. Definition of marketing strategy will always remain a creative process; however, it may prove necessary to define guidelines which go beyond standard marketing theory in order to guide companies in making this choice.

FIGURE 8.2

Benefits dependency network: simplified example (A&P = advertising and promotion)

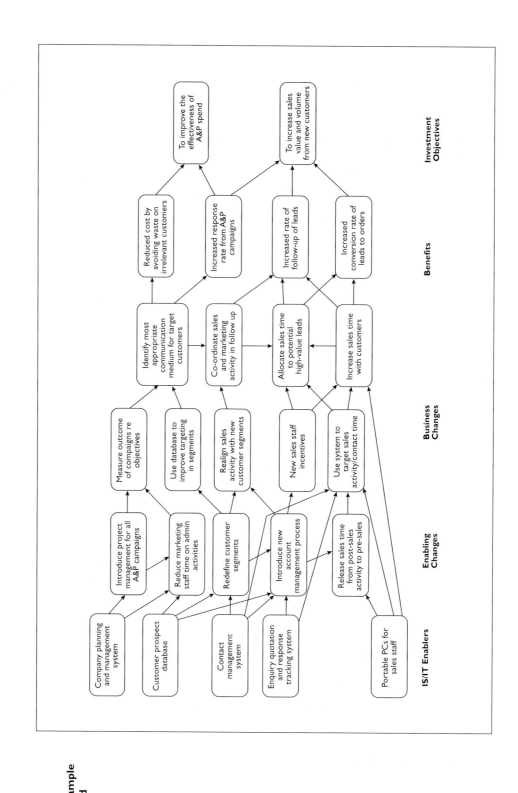

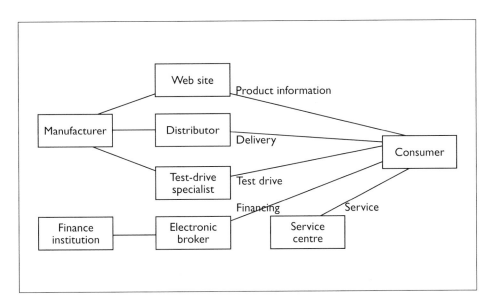

FIGURE 8.3

Separating physical and informational logic: car retailing

Summary

The interrelationship between these five research questions is shown in Figure 8.4.

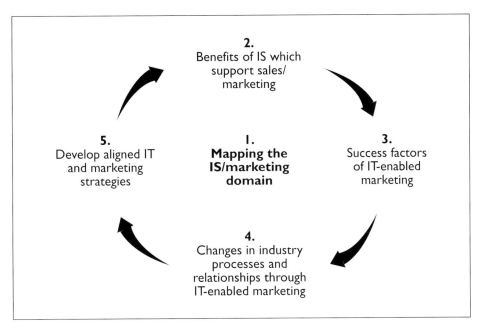

FIGURE 8.4

Questions for future research

We have presented in this report our initial findings in some of these areas. Nevertheless, the views of practitioners we have reported in this chapter show that further research in this vital area of marketing practice is much needed.

Appendix A

Expert respondents

In compiling this report, 12 experts in the field were interviewed to complement the authors' literature review and the case studies. Drawn both from Cranfield School of Management's community of researchers, consultants and lecturers and from outside Cranfield, the interviewees are listed below.

Professor Martin Christopher is Head of the Marketing and Logistics Faculty and Chairman of the Centre for Logistics and Transportation at Cranfield School of Management. He is also Deputy Director of the School, responsible for Executive Development Programmes. His recent books have focused on relationship marketing, customer service and logistics strategy.

Dr Roger Elvin is a lecturer in Information Systems, having joined Cranfield from the British Standards Institution where he was the Head of Corporate IT Services. He has worked in IS/IT for 25 years in a variety of management and consultancy roles. His previous employers include Goodyear, Esso Chemicals, Unilever, Logica and the Civil Aviation Authority.

Professor Keith Fletcher is Dean of the School of Management at the University of East Anglia. Formerly Professor of Marketing at the University of Strathclyde, he is author of *Marketing Management and Information Technology*, a wide-ranging and comprehensive review of the field.

Professor Kit Grindley is a long-standing and influential observer of the computing industry and its effect on business. Author of a seminal work on the relationship between the IT function and the rest of the organisation, *Managing IT at Board Level*, Kit Grindley is a Visiting Professor of Systems Automation at London School of Economics.

Nick Hewson has worked in the field of IT in marketing for many years, and is the author of a number of practitioner reports on the subject. With Wendy Hewson he now runs Hewson Consulting Group, a consultancy providing independent advice on IT-enabled marketing, and Sistrum, the UK's dominant research club of companies with an interest in the area, with an increasing Net-enabled membership of overseas organisations.

Sean Kelly is author of the two leading books on data warehousing. After a career to date spanning management consultancy, general management and software engineering, he now runs the Data Warehouse Network, a consortium of organisations working together to learn how to use databases for maximum marketing leverage. His influence on the sponsorship and implementation models frequently used in data warehousing projects is widely acknowledged.

Peter Mouncey is General Manager, Group Marketing Services at the AA, where his responsibilities include customer database services in addition to market research, new product development and marketing planning. He is ex-Chairman of both the Market Research Society and the Association of Users of Research Agencies. He is currently Chairman of the Research Development Foundation of the market research industry, and is a Visiting Fellow of Cranfield University.

Joe Peppard is a Research Fellow at Cranfield School of Management and a lecturer at Trinity College Dublin. Editor of *IT Strategy for Business* and author of numerous articles, he has expertise in electronic commerce, executive information systems, business re-engineering and IT-enabled change, and the IT/business relationship.

Lynette Ryals is a Teaching Fellow in Cranfield's Marketing Group. After working as an investment manager, leading the investment tables and successfully launching new products, she worked for a large management consultancy before moving to Cranfield, where she has advised numerous clients on all aspects of marketing strategy. She is currently conducting research on IT-enabled customer relationship management, and a long-term study of the measurement of customer profitability and its application.

Professor Robert Shaw is a leading independent observer of IT in marketing. At Andersen Consulting and, more recently, with Shaw Consulting, he has published several influential reports on the subject and consulted widely to UK and international organisations. He is currently researching the vital related topic of measuring marketing effectiveness. He is a Visiting Professor at Cranfield School of Management.

Sri Srikanthan is a lecturer in the Accounting and Finance Group at Cranfield, and Director of Cranfield's Marketing Accounting Research Centre. He has worked with numerous sponsoring companies developing accounting information systems for marketing decisions and has written extensively on the subject. He also lectures on the financial measurement of marketing investments.

Professor John Ward is Professor of Strategic Information Systems and Director of the Information Systems Research Centre at Cranfield. He is co-author of the books *Strategic Planning for Information Systems* and *The Essence of Information Systems*. He consults to a number of large organisations on the development and implementation of IS/IT strategies.

Bibliography

Acey, M. (1997) 'Snail mail to "die within a decade"', *The Times*, 3 September.

Aitken, S. and Bintley, H. (1989) 'Building a marketeer's workbench: an expert system applied to the marketing planning process', *ICL Technical Journal*, November, 721–36.

Alpar, P. (1991) 'Knowledge-based modeling of marketing managers' problem solving behaviour', *International Journal of Research in Marketing*, 8 (1), 5–16.

Andersen Consulting (1989) *IT in Marketing and Sales '89*. London: Andersen Consulting.

Arinze, B. (1990) 'Market planning with computer models: a case study in the software industry', *Industrial Marketing Management*, 19, 117–29.

Arnold, M.E. and Penn, J.M. (1987) 'The information technology revolution in marketing (1): a review of some current applications', *Quarterly Review of Marketing*, January, 1–7.

Barker, V. and O'Connor, D. (1989) 'Expert systems for configuration at Digital: XCON and beyond', *Communications of the ACM*, 32 (3), 298–318.

Bartlett, C.A. and Goshal, S. (1995) 'Changing the role of top management: beyond systems to people', *Harvard Business Review*, May–June, 132–42.

Bayer, J. and Harter, R. (1991) '"Miner", "manager", and "researcher": three modes of analysis of scanner data', *International Journal of Research in Marketing*, 8 (1), 17–27.

Black, G. (1999) 'Pressure to combine web and call centre technologies', *Financial Times*, 3 February.

Blattberg, R. and Deighton, J. (1991) 'Interactive marketing: exploiting the age of addressability', *Sloan Management Review*.

Blodgett, M. (1997) 'Ordering errors to go home', *Computerworld*, 31 (11), 2.

Borch, O.J. and Hartvigsen, G. (1991) 'Knowledge-based systems for strategic market planning in small firms', *Decision Support Systems*, 7, 145–57.

Brady, J. and Davis, I. (1993) 'Marketing in transition: marketing's mid-life crisis', *McKinsey Quarterly*, 2, 17–28.

Buttery A. and Tamaschke R. (1995) 'Marketing decision support systems in a small trading nation: an Australian case study', *Marketing Intelligence and Planning*, 13 (2), 14–27.

Cairncross, F. (1997) *The Death of Distance: How the communications revolution will change our lives*. London: Orion Business Books.

Cambridge Technology Group (1998) *UK Organisations Fail to Grasp New Internet Opportunities*. Cambridge Technology Group, Cambridge, MA.

Cook, D.A. and Sterling, J.W. (1989) 'Alacrity: software that asks shrewd questions', *Planning Review*, November–December, 22–7.

Cooper, R.G. (1981) 'An empirically derived new product project selection model', *IEEE Transactions on Engineering Management*, 28 (3), 54–61.

Cope, N. (1999) 'Internet book deal boosts WH Smith', *The Independent*, 16 January.

Daisley, S. (1997) 'Going for the one', *New Perspectives*, 9, 13–16.

Dandurand, L. (1993) 'A computer-based technology structure for international marketing strategy development', *Journal of Strategic Marketing*, 1, 141–52.

Datamation (1997) 'Sales automation product is Internet-aware', *Datamation*, February, 24.

Denton, N. (1997) 'Insurance on the net: Ripe for transformation', *Financial Times*, 2 July.

Dragoon, A. (1995) 'A force to be reckoned with', *CIO*, 8 (18), 54–5.

Duan, Y. and Burrell, P. (1995) 'A hybrid system for strategic marketing planning', *Marketing Intelligence and Planning*, 13 (11), 5–12.

Dubelaar, C., Finlay, P.N. and Tylor, D. (1991) 'Expert systems: the cold fusion of marketing?', *Journal of Marketing Management*, 7, 371–82.

Economist (1994) 'Death of the brand manager', editorial, *The Economist*, 9 April, 79–80.

Economist (1997) 'On-line retailing: web browsing', *The Economist*, 29 March, 97–8.

Eden, C. (1989) 'Using cognitive mapping for strategic options development and analysis (SODA)', in Rosenhead, J. (ed.), *Rational Analysis for a Problematic World*. Chichester: Wiley, pp. 21–42.

Eisenhart, T. (1990) 'After 10 years of marketing decision support systems, where's the payoff?', *Business Marketing*, June, 46–51.

Evans, P.B. and Wurster, T.S. (1997) 'Strategy and the new economics of information', *Harvard Business Review*, September–October, 71–82.

Fletcher, K. (1995) *Marketing Management and Information Technology*, 2nd edn. Hemel Hempstead: Prentice Hall.

Foremski, T. (1997) 'Online answers in seconds on new mortgage inquiries', *Financial Times*, 2 July.

Freeman, E. (1997) 'Datamining unearths dollars', *Datamation*, July, 84–8.

Gens, F. (1999) Paper at *IDC Directions 99*, San Francisco. Quoted in *Computing*, 11 March, 16.

Goodchild, M.F. (1991) 'Geographic information systems', *Journal of Retailing*, 67 (1), 3–15.

Gorski, D. (1993) 'Sales and marketing systems – a real way to achieve competitive advantage', in McDonald, M.H.B., Hewson, W. and Wilson, H.N. (eds), *Emerging Information Technologies – A Marketing Opportunity*. Milton Keynes: HCG Publications.

Greco, A.J. and Hogue, J.T. (1990) 'Developing marketing decision support systems in consumer goods firms', *Journal of Consumer Marketing*, 7 (1), 55–63.

Griffith, V. (1997) 'Freedom fantasy: an interview with Stephen Roach', *Financial Times*, 13 August.

Grindley, K. (1995) '*Managing IT at Board Level*, 2nd edn. London: FT Pitman.

Hair, J.F. and Keep, W.W. (1997) 'Electronic marketing: future possibilities', in Peterson, R.A. (ed.), *Electronic Marketing and the Consumer*. Thousand Oaks, CA: Sage.

Hewson, N. and Hewson, W. (1994) *The Impact of Computerised Sales and Marketing Systems in the UK*, 4th edn. Milton Keynes: HCG Publications.

Hewson, W. and Wilson, H.N. (1994) 'Exploring the alignment of information technology investments with sales and marketing strategies', in *Proceedings of British Academy of Management Annual Conference*, Management School, Lancaster University, 372–3.

Hill, K. (1997) 'Electronic marketing: the Dell Computer experience', in Peterson, R.A. (ed.), *Electronic Marketing and the Consumer*, Thousand Oaks, CA: Sage.

Hirst, M. (1991a) 'Personal computer software for use in marketing education, Part 1', *Journal of Marketing Management*, 7, 77–92.

Hirst, M. (1991b) 'Personal computer software for use in marketing education, Part 2', *Journal of Marketing Management*, 7, 167–88.

Holtham, C. (1993) 'Groupware in marketing', in McDonald, M.H.B., Hewson, W. and Wilson, H.N. (eds), *Emerging Information Technologies – A Marketing Opportunity*. Milton Keynes: HCG Publications.

Hoptroff, R.G. (1992) 'The principles and practice of time series forecasting and business modelling using neural nets', in *Neural Computing Applications*, 1 (1), London: Springer-Verlag.

Jarvenpaa, S.L. and Todd, P.A. (1997) 'Is there a future for retailing on the Net?', in Peterson, R.A. (ed.), *Electronic Marketing and the Consumer*. Thousand Oaks, CA: Sage, pp. 139–54.

Jolson, M.A. and Rossow, G.L. (1971) 'The Delphi process in marketing decision making', *Journal of Marketing Research*, November, 443–8.

Kavanagh, J. (1999) 'Case study: Charles Schwab', *Financial Times*, 3 February.

Kavanagh, M. (1997) 'The times is a'changing under NI Internet chief', *Marketing Week*, 3 July, 29.

Kim, H. (1997) 'Internet customer service', *Business Computer World*, September, 53–6.

Lamb, J. (1997a) 'Late-night soul search over SAP', *Computing*, 26 June, 18.

Lamb, J. (1997b) 'Harnessing the data deluge', *Computing*, 25 September, 10.

Lea, G. (1997) 'Net success for Digital', *Computing*, 9 October.

Lee, H.G. (1998) 'Do electronic marketplaces lower the price of goods?', *Communications of the ACM*, 41 (1), 73–80.

Lennox, G. (1993) 'An intelligent approach to integrating marketing databases with other technologies', in McDonald, M.H.B., Hewson, W. and Wilson, H.N. (eds), *Emerging Information Technologies – A Marketing Opportunity*. Milton Keynes: HCG Publications.

Little, J.D.C. (1970) 'Models and managers: the concept of a decision calculus', *Management Science*, 16 (8), B466–85.

Lockett, A. and Littler, D. (1997) 'The adoption of direct banking services', *Journal of Marketing Management*, 13, 791–816.

Lodish, L.M. (1981) 'Experience with decision-calculus models and decision support systems', in Schultz, R.L. and Zoltners, A.A. (eds), *Marketing Decision Models*. Amsterdam: Elsevier.

Magretta, J. (1998) 'The power of virtual integration: an interview with Dell Computers' Michael Dell', *Harvard Business Review*, 73–84.

Manchester, P. (1997) 'Virtual finance: the market is wide open', *Financial Times*, 2 July.

Marsh, P. (1996) 'Picked out by programs', *Financial Times*, 24 May.

McCann, J. M. (1991) 'Expert systems in marketing', *International Journal of Research in Marketing*, 8 (1), 1–3.

McDonald, M.H.B. (1989b) 'Marketing planning and expert systems: an epistemology of practice', *Marketing Intelligence and Planning*, 7 (7/8), 16–23.

McDonald, M.H.B. and Dunbar, I. (1995) *Market Segmentation: A Step-by-Step Approach to Creating Profitable Market Segments*. London: Macmillan.

McDonald, M.H.B. and Wilson, H.N. (1990) 'State-of-the-art developments in expert systems and strategic marketing planning', *British Journal of Management*, 1, 159–70.

McDonald, M.H.B and Wilson, H.N. (1993) 'Why apply software to marketing strategy? Mapping the sources of competitive advantage', in McDonald, M.H.B., Hewson, W. and Wilson, H.N. (eds), *Emerging Information Technologies – A Marketing Opportunity*. Milton Keynes: HCG Publications.

McDonald, M.H.B., Denison, T. and Ryals, L. (1994) *Marketing: The Challenge of Change*. Maidenhead: Chartered Institute of Marketing.

McDonald, M.H.B., Hewson, W. and Wilson, H.N. (eds) (1993) *Emerging Information Technologies – A Marketing Opportunity*. Milton Keynes: HCG Publications.

McDonald, M.H.B., Wilson, H.N. and Hewson, W. (1996) *Towards Excellence in Marketing Strategy: The Role of Systems in Strategic Marketing and Business Planning*. Milton Keynes: HCG Publications.

McNeilly, M. and Gessner, S. (1993) 'Business Insight: an expert system for strategic analysis', *Planning Review*, March/April.

Moody, G. (1997) 'Up the Amazon', *Business Computer World*, September, 106–7.

Morgan, N.A. and Piercy, N.F. (1993) 'Increasing planning effectiveness', *Management Decision*, 31 (4), 55–8.

Moriarty, R.T. and Swartz, G.S. (1989) 'Automation to boost sales and marketing', *Harvard Business Review*, 67 (1), 100–108.

Morris, M.H., Burns, A.C. and Avila, R.A. (1989) 'Computer awareness and usage by industrial marketers', *Industrial Marketing Management*, 18 (3), 223–32.

Newing, R. (1995) 'Marketing Director: marketing made easy', *Management Consultancy*, April.

Norusis, M.J. (1993) *SPSS for Windows Base System User's Guide*, release 6.0. Chicago, IL: SPSS, Inc.

Nyce, J.M. and Kahn, P. (eds) (1992) *From Memex to Hypertext: Vannevar Bush and the Mind's Machine*. London: Academic Press.

O'Brien, R.C. (1991) 'EIS and strategic control', *Long Range Planning*, 24 (5), 125–7.

O'Connor, J. and Galvin, E. (1997) *Marketing and Information Technology*. London: Pitman.

Ovum (1997) *Ovum Evaluates ERP for Manufacturers*. London: Ovum.

Peacock, P.R. (1998) 'Data mining in marketing, part 1', *Marketing Management*, Winter, 9–18.

Peppard, J. (1998) 'Competing on the Web: winning in the new consumer marketplace', draft paper, Cranfield School of Management.

Perry, C. and Euler, T. (1989) 'Marketing simulations in tertiary institutions: a review and future directions', *European Journal of Marketing*, 23 (4), 40–49.

Peterson, C.R. (1994) 'Software review: HIVIEW', *OR/MS Today*, April.

Phillips, D. (1993) 'Abbey National Direct – creating a future with information and marketing technology', in McDonald, M.H.B., Hewson, W. and Wilson, H.N. (eds), *Emerging Information Technologies – A Marketing Opportunity*. Milton Keynes: HCG Publications.

Phillips, F. et al. (1997) 'Electronically connecting retailers and customers: interim summary of an expert roundtable', in Peterson, R.A. (ed.), *Electronic Marketing and the Consumer*, Thousand Oaks, CA: Sage, pp. 101–22.

Phillips, L. (1989) 'People-centred group decision support', in Doukidis, G.I., Land, F. and Miller, G. (eds), *Knowledge-Based Management Support Systems*. Chichester: Ellis Horwood, pp. 208–24.

Piercy, N.F. (1989) 'Information control and the power and politics of marketing', *Journal of Business Research*, 18, 229–43.

Price, C. (1999) 'Vital links in the chain of supply', *Financial Times*, 10 February.

Proctor, R.A. (1992) 'Marketing decision support systems: a role for neural networking', *Marketing Intelligence and Planning*, 10 (1), 21–6.

Proctor, R.A. (1995) 'Marketing planning: a computer assisted approach', *Marketing Intelligence and Planning*, 13 (7), 7–12.

Rangaswamy, A., Harlam, B.A. and Lodish, L.M. (1991) 'INFER: an expert system for automatic analysis of scanner data', *International Journal of Research in Marketing*, 8 (1), 29–40.

Rangaswamy, A., Eliashberg, J., Burke, R.R. and Wind, J. (1989) 'Developing marketing expert systems: an application to international negotiations', *Journal of Marketing*, 53, 24–39.

Ranger, S. (1999) 'Net shoppers face world wide wait', *Computing*, 11 March, 3.

Reed, D. (1996) 'Streets ahead', *Marketing Week*, 17 May.

Rees-Mogg, W. (1997) 'Is Bill Gates really selling us all Ladas?', *The Times*, 15 December, 20.

Reichheld, F.F. and Sasser, W.E. Jr (1990) 'Zero defections: quality comes to services', *Harvard Business Review*, September–October, 105–11.

Robertson, C. (1997a) 'What's in store', *Computing*, 6 March, 46.

Robertson, C. (1997b) 'Online shopping – retail revolution or technological blind alley?', *Computing*, 7 August, 16.

Sabbagh, D. (1997) 'Bankers count the cost', *Computing*, 16 October.

Semanoff, M. (1996) 'Meeting the challenge of contact management', *Industrial Distribution*, 85 (11), T16–T25.

Shaw, R. (1991) *The Sales and Marketing Systems Report*. London: Shaw Consulting.

Shaw, R. (1994) *How to Transform Marketing Through IT*. London: Business Intelligence.

Sheth, J.N. and Sisodia, R.S. (1997) 'Consumer behaviour in the future', in Peterson, R.A. (ed.), *Electronic Marketing and the Consumer*. Thousand Oaks, CA: Sage, pp. 17–38.

Sleight, P. (1997) 'Lifestyle, the universe and everything', *New Perspectives*, 9, 6.

Snoddy, R. (1999) 'EMI tackles Net threat', *The Times*, 8 February.

Soane, A. (1997) 'Web site reports', *Business Computer World*, September, 87.

Stone, R.W. and Good, D.J. (1995) 'Expert systems in the marketing organisation', *Industrial Management and Data Systems*, 95 (4), 3–7.

Taylor, P. (1997) 'The race is on', *Financial Times*, 2 July.

Travis, A. (1999) 'Poll points to lift off for Internet', *The Guardian*, 11 January.

Tull, D.S. and Hawkins, D.I. (1984) *Marketing Research: Measurement and Method*, 3rd edn. New York: Macmillan.

Vernon, M. (1999) 'It's still an uphill struggle', *Financial Times*, 3 February.

Waalewijn, P. and Boulan, R. (1990) 'Strategic planning on a personal computer', *Long Range Planning*, 23 (4), 97–103.

Wiley, J.B. (1989) 'Four time series analysis packages', *Journal of Marketing Research*, February, 129–33.

Wilson, H.N. (1989) 'EXMAR: automating marketing planning', *Proceedings, Fifth International Expert Systems Conference*, June. London: Learned Information, 157–68.

Wilson, H.N. (1990) 'Hypertext: extending the software toolbox to assist information workers', *Software Tools 90 Conference*, London, June. London: Learned Information.

Wilson, H.N. and McDonald, M.H.B. (1994a) 'Decision support systems as learning aids: the case of marketing planning', refereed paper, *Proceedings of the Marketing Education Group Annual Conference*, University of Ulster, 1028–37.

Wilson, H.N. and McDonald, M.H.B. (1994b) 'Critical problems in marketing planning: the potential of decision support systems', *Journal of Strategic Marketing*, 2, 249–69.

Wilson, H.N. and McDonald, M.H.B. (1996) 'Computer aided marketing planning: the experience of early adopters', *Journal of Marketing Management*, 12, 391–416.

Wright, G. and Rowe, G. (1992) 'Expert systems in marketing: current trends and an alternative scenario', *Marketing Intelligence and Planning*, 10 (6), 24–30.

Index